THE
NAKED
TRUTH

THE
NAKED
TRUTH

Reclaiming Sexual Freedom
in a Culture of Lies

CYNTHIA GARRETT

REGNERY
FAITH

Scriptures marked ESV are taken from ESV® Bible (The Holy Bible, English Standard Version®), copyright © 2001 by Crossway, a publishing ministry of Good News Publishers. Used by permission. All rights reserved.

Scriptures marked NIV are taken from the Holy Bible, New International Version®, NIV®. Copyright © 1973, 1978, 1984, 2011 by Biblica, Inc.® Used by permission of Zondervan. All rights reserved worldwide. www.zondervan.com. The "NIV" and "New International Version" are trademarks registered in the United States Patent and Trademark Office by Biblica, Inc.®

Scripture quotations marked NKJV are taken from the New King James Version.® Copyright © 1982 by Thomas Nelson. Used by permission. All rights reserved.

Scriptures marked NLT are taken from the Holy Bible, New Living Translation. Copyright © 1996, 2004, 2015 by Tyndale House Foundation. Used by permission of Tyndale House Ministries, Carol Stream, Illinois 60188. All rights reserved.

Regnery Faith books may be purchased in bulk at special discounts for sales promotion, corporate gifts, fund-raising, or educational purposes. Special editions can also be created to specifications. For details, contact the Special Sales Department, Regnery Faith, 307 West 36th Street, 11th Floor, New York, NY 10018 or info@skyhorsepublishing.com.

Regnery Faith™ is an imprint of Skyhorse Publishing, Inc.®, a Delaware corporation.

Visit our website at www.regnery.com.
Please follow our publisher Tony Lyons on Instagram @tonylyonsisuncertain.

10 9 8 7 6 5 4 3 2 1
Library of Congress Cataloging-in-Publication Data is available on file.

Cover design by John Caruso
Cover photo by Matt Beard

Print ISBN: 978-1-68451-371-0
Ebook ISBN: 978-1-5107-8156-6

Printed in the United States

CONTENTS

To my husband, Roger

Thank you for teaching me every day how valuable I am.
You have shown me countless times what Jesus looks like.
Your walk with the Lord is an example to everyone we meet.
This entire book is dedicated to you and the life of faith we have
built and continue to build daily.

FOREWORD

The first thing you notice about Cynthia Garrett when you meet her is her extraordinary, exotic beauty. But then, when you begin to engage her in conversation, you discover a very serious and deep intelligence. And finally, you realize that you are actually looking at a very special and anointed woman of God.

Her story is as unusual as she is, and in her book *The Naked Truth*, Cynthia reveals the journey she has been on for decades, both personally and professionally, from promiscuity to purity. The more you learn about Cynthia, the more you grow to admire and respect this woman who is far more beautiful than she even first appeared. For there is much to learn from Cynthia, because everything she says is based on her own personal experience in a world that exists solely to worship at the altar of beauty and ambition and success—served up, of course, with a great deal of sexuality. Cynthia speaks the truth in a spirit of love and without condemnation.

I have grown to love my fascinating friend for the beauty she radiates from the Savior that she loves with all her soul.

You will love her too, and hopefully you will find your own beautiful self in the story she so powerfully shares.

—Kathie Lee Gifford, March 2024

Introduction

SEX AND PURITY IN AN IMPURE WORLD

T here is a naked truth about sex. A truth many never want you to find. A truth our entire society is *invested* in your not finding. Why? Because these people want your complicity. They want your support, your acceptance, or your avoidance of this truth, and they want you to hide your head in the sand of your very busy life. By doing so, you are perhaps not paying attention to a world of chaos that surrounds the entire universe of sex and sexuality.

What do we do? Whose opinion matters? How do we navigate sex and sexuality in an impure world? *What is the naked truth about our nakedness?*

In my twenties, I was given my own late-night show on the NBC network. I was young, wealthy, and successful. I thought I had hit the lotto of my dreams, and certainly the dream of millions of young women like me.

One day I was hiking around my home in West Hollywood with a girlfriend of mine. I was confused about how unhappy I felt despite having a career I loved; having eligible, successful, even famous men interested in me; and owning a closet Carrie Bradshaw would have died for. (More on Carrie Bradshaw later.) As we were talking about our sex lives, she shared with me her "six-week rule."

When I asked her what she meant by a six-week rule, she simply replied, "A lot happens in six weeks, and if he waits, maybe he is worth my time. Maybe not. But I give myself time to see more clearly."

The wisdom of this struck me like a lightning bolt. I knew exactly what she meant. And I was immediately dumbfounded—at *myself*. Even though I called myself a Christian, I had no rules at all about dating, much less about sex. Truthfully, I didn't view sex as sacred. By that point in my life, I didn't even view sex as important, apart from getting the commitment I wanted, or in some cases actually enjoying the experience.

I just did what I felt my heart told me to do. "Following my heart" seemed like freedom to me. I felt empowered and liberated by being able to do what I wanted with my own body. I knew God had things to say about sex in the Bible, but I found biblical rules ambiguous enough to not deal with in a real way—and honestly, I preferred to keep it that way. As long as any understanding of my Christian faith as it related to sex was ambiguous, I could live in the gray and make rules that seemed good for me. After all, I had been sexually molested in my past, and I deserved to be the one making rules about my own body.

When listening to my friend, however, I was impressed at the self-respect a boundary like hers required. I also realized that if

I had waited even six weeks to sleep with any guy I had dated, I would never have slept with any of them at all!

In hindsight, I was giving myself away and calling it love. It always *felt* like love. And I loved the feeling of being in love and falling in love. The entire chase of it all was exhilarating. The game for me was just a desperate plea to be loved—to be seen and honored. Following the old saying "Women use sex for love and men use love for sex," I now understand that I was simply using my body as the ultimate bargaining chip.

I was certain that no man I was dating would have tolerated waiting six weeks for me. That should have told me how little they valued me or how little I valued myself. But to be honest, the feeling was mutual. I didn't value the guys enough either to wait six weeks for them. We were using each other, and sex was usually one of the reasons why.

A hard look at myself revealed I was chasing flesh, and if the pursuit of someone felt exciting enough, I didn't have the ability to wait even six minutes—much less six weeks.

But this was how every modern woman I knew lived. The women I looked up to were rich, famous, and beautiful. I felt like I was in an elite club of empowered, feminist-minded, sexually liberated, successful women. I wanted what I wanted NOW, and my impurity and my impatience were doing major damage to my mind, my soul, and my life—not to mention my heart.

Yet, I believed I was a good Christian girl at heart.

Like many of you reading right now, I dare say that *love* is the goal for most of you, but that doesn't fit the role you often play while trying to get the opposite sex interested in you. You, like most people, have shifted your focus to make your relationships revolve around your desire for pleasure, and love be damned, because *love* isn't even on the table.

What's on the table is the opportunity to be perceived as "cool," "empowered," and "sex-positive" by playing the game provided to us in the guise of sexual liberation. This sexual acceptance of "it's all good" has been crafted to be seen as the powerful attitude reflected in every image, everywhere around us. We cannot let on that we want "more," or we will be seen as weak. Women must do specific sexual things to get the guy—and keep him interested. Men must appear aloof and disconnected to keep the modern woman interested. In reality, we are all being truly destroyed because we are not getting what we really want—or *need*.

We all want *love* and are too afraid to admit it. So, we often use sex as a tool for momentary glimpses of something beautiful and far more sacred.

For women, in short—thanks to the Sexual Revolution—we are now free to abuse ourselves the way men once did! But if you consider yourself a feminist, you must ask yourself if this male-dominated culture is still simply dominating us?

From abortion to birth control to the trans movement, men have simply taken our female identity and twisted and manipulated us into sex toys and idiots by making us think we are empowering ourselves with our own sexual freedom. We are really destroying ourselves by playing a game created to satisfy man's sexual appetite. And although we have developed an appetite as women, our appetite is wired to receive love and commitment—and that's not happening in our culture today.

All the games around sex and sexuality for me—especially because I appeared to be a winner in the game—were just a good shield to hide my low self-esteem and my need to have power over my heart and mind. Broken by past childhood trauma, relationship after relationship, experience after experience, time after time, my heart and mind were just as troubled after the sex was over. I was left just as lonely, just as angry, just as confused, and feeling just as unseen. I was tortured inside knowing I was being taken without anything satisfying to my soul being given in return.

Perhaps this explains why sex and sexuality today feel *cheap*. You know in some way you are being played and sold for less than you are worth. Sex and sexuality feel like a device, a trap, a game. They have become a marketing tool, a political tool, and a mechanism for control—especially control of women and the freedoms we think we have won. We are told there is power in our freedom to say yes. What nobody is telling you is that there is bondage in your yes—and power in your NO!

The truth is that sex is meant to be sacred! It is meant to be beautiful and amazing. It is meant to create oneness and unity. It is meant to be shared in a safe space. But the only way this can happen is if we can restore its beauty by explaining its actual purpose and power in our lives. This is why I hope you are here, reading this book. This is my goal. I want to help you understand that, as many feminists around the globe are now learning, there are no safe spaces outside monogamy and commitment.

It is time for a revolutionary look at sex and sexuality. As they relate to all of us at various stages of life and as they relate to our identity, we need to understand their sacredness. We are drowning in a sea of confusion, and men profit the most from women who, when drowning, naturally cling to the men for support. If there are no real men to cling to, what happens? And what is a real man, or a real woman, anyway?

In our "swipe right" culture, intimacy is all but non-existent. So getting to what's real is becoming harder and harder for those plugged in to "the Matrix." Gaining sexual freedom is completely possible when you say no to a culture built on casual sex. The question is . . . how do we do this?

The pursuit of sex alone—or unsacred sex, as I call it—has tremendous power for evil. Why? Because at best it is a motivation for sex without commitment or honesty. At its worst, it motivates some to violence, rape, lies, and abuses while leaving others damaged and broken for life.

Identity Has Nothing to Do with Sex and Sexuality

We see everywhere that today's sexuality sows much confusion, especially when it is mistaken for *identity*. This confusion has produced fringe groups that wage battles against us, our children, and ultimately against themselves because they want their sexuality and their sexual choices affirmed in the way that we accept people's identities, races, or nationalities. This can never happen because anyone with half a brain knows that sex and sexuality have nothing to do with identity. I am Cynthia, Bernard Sr. and Linda Garrett's daughter. I am a minister, a writer, a TV personality, a wife, a mom, a daughter, a sister. I am also a natural-born heterosexual female. These are all things I do and am. They are not my identity. My identity is simple. I am Cynthia, God's creation.

For example, I knew intuitively when at the top of my career as a network TV host that that had nothing to do with who I really was. It's what I *did*. I began dreaming of working on TV when I was around five years old. Yet even at one year old, I was already who I am today. I was me from the day I was born. I am still me, and my behavior can never change that. Locked inside your choices, your actions, and your behaviors—you too are still *you*. The you you've been from the day you were born.

If your behavior determined who you are, I know many parents who would have given up on their prodigal children years ago. Yet what parent says, "My kid is just a drug addict, or a liar, or a thief, or even a murderer, because that's just who they are?" Any parent knows their child's behavior can change. And that's why all parents hold out hope for their children.

I too hold out hope for our society. I hope that we can see the need to look deeply at sex and sexuality and ask some tough questions.

Even though we know the emperor is naked, sex and sexuality, no matter how confused, are being prettied up on the outside by wealth or political agendas to appear glamorous and aspirational, even inspirational—minus all the things that make them sacred. Minus the love, the commitment, the safety, and the intimacy.

For both sexes, this means an inner landscape saturated in self-pleasure—a landscape actively hostile to intimacy, ruled by shame and pain, and governed by a false belief that male and female sexuality are the same. Sadly, the pursuit of pleasure becomes a degraded search for thrills—one which leaves both sexes numb and jaded, scarred by having traded in real love and respect for being demeaned.

Because sex has become so distorted from what it should be, and was created to be, everything we've made it become is violence against our psyche, our stability, our youth, and our futures.

Christians are supposed to understand the importance of sex and why God says it is for the marriage bed, since it is clearly written out for us in the Bible. Yet many believers are indistinguishable from their unbelieving friends. Some, if not worse than their unbelieving friends, are certainly *worse off* because an act against your faith leaves you in constant inner turmoil. Don't I remember that turmoil!

Statistics say that over 95 percent of people have sex outside of marriage. According to statistics from Women's Health Interactive, "By the age of 44, 95% of survey respondents reported having premarital sex, and about two-thirds of the American public views it as acceptable."[1]

According to a Pew Research survey, "half of Christians interviewed say casual sex, defined in the survey as sex between consenting adults who are not in a committed romantic relationship, is sometimes or always acceptable. Six in ten Catholics (62%) take this view, as do 56% of Protestants in the historically Black tradition, 54% of mainline Protestants, and 36% of evangelical Protestants."[2]

A general manager of a Hilton hotel told me a story one year that was even more shocking. He claimed that the highest rate of pornography sold on their in-room TVs occurred when the Christian conference was in town yearly.

Sadly, many Christians have completely blended into the social norms created by everyone else. We don't hold our line. We don't consider sex sacred. We don't do anything except complain about how immoral other people's *lifestyles* are while not really providing a shining example of purity that others are drawn to.

We have all lost our way. But many Christians have lost their way *and* compromised their faith through their acceptance of "anything and everything goes" when it comes to sex and sexuality in the name of "*love*." But this is a confused form of love that doesn't at all resemble God's love.

An outside look at sex and sexuality in America today is like looking down Alice's rabbit hole. It is crazy and dark. It is confusing madness that resembles the scene in the city center of *The Hunger Games*. Everyone is gender fluid. No one is completely male or female. Sexuality is mistakenly perceived as identity. There is a skulking air of sex everywhere. And children are no longer off limits.

My Introduction to Sex: The Connection

Sex for me began prematurely and horrifyingly. I was sexually abused as a child by a close family member. This made sex and sexuality scary to me. I dreaded him lying in the dark, touching me inappropriately while I pretended to be asleep, paralyzed with fear and confusion.

This abuse destroyed my security, my innocence, and my understanding of what sex could and should be for many years. Every sex act—consensual or otherwise—leaves an intangible mark on your mind and spirit. This one left me with bruises and scars that have now become the deep well from which I help others become free. I understand deep down in that well what it feels like to box with those ghosts.

His actions, I later realized, were sexual and for him alone. He never considered me or the damage to me that he was causing. He never thought about the twisted path he was providing me to walk on regarding sex and my own sexuality. I did not matter to him. His desires in the moment mattered. This is what sex without any understanding or regard for its sacredness does to people. It causes a disgusting selfish greed that will feed on anything it can—especially children. Children make the easiest targets because we are too innocent to know what's happening, too scared to say a word, and too powerless to have a voice.

This kind of selfish sexuality never cares about its victims. And sadly, it comes up in consensual relationships as well. It seeks to feed and satisfy itself for its own pleasure. Some will lie for it, cheat for it, and harm others for it.

As a need to survive, and in an attempt to thrive, I learned quickly to make sex a satisfying and selfish thing also. After I turned sixteen years old, since I had been inappropriately sexualized by abuse at an early age, sexual attraction was a major preoccupation for me.

I thought I had to use sex as a bargaining tool to get what I wanted. Since I could give it and take it away, I could experience it with whomever I chose because, as a young adult—short of rape—nobody could force me to lie in fear *again* while they took what they wanted from me.

I learned to protect myself under the guise of being a sexually liberated person. I learned how to dress and look the part of a sexually in-control, powerful, and desirable young woman. Shows like *Sex and the City* affirmed my belief in my ability to do what I wanted with whomever I wanted sexually. The media said I was free to be—sexually. And so, I was.

For many years, I lived in a state of mind that I call "revenge sex." I used my sexual exploits to try and make amends for my stolen innocence, power, security, and trust. I pursued sexiness and desirability as a means of self-protection and control over men. I learned to essentially disconnect my head and heart from my body. Each time a man took from my essence without so much as a care, I dug my feet in to my will to win at this game.

Empowered by voices in the media and culture, I thought I was liberated to be the captain of my own body and navigate it in any way I saw fit for my pleasure. Even abortion was within reason because why should anyone make me have a baby when I didn't want the father? And vice versa. Just as sex was not sacred, the things that came with sex were not either. Babies, marriage, commitment, and monogamy were all consequences that did not need to exist in a sexually free world where consenting adults did whatever they wanted with each other.

Honestly, in my twenties and thirties I didn't know much about the Sexual Revolution or the feminist movements. I only knew the words they used seemed to affirm my need to self-protect and my choice to be the one who said yes and no over my body. That empowered me as I struggled to find my identity and voice, long lost and silenced in a dark room by my abuser.

Sex came to occupy a territory of my life that I really did not understand at all. In not seeing it as sacred, I was free to engage in it with whomever I chose. But even as I thought I was using sex to dominate others while protecting my own heart, my enjoyment of what we are created to enjoy, and my deep yearning for real love and healing, eventually made it an idol. And eventually I worshiped the idol. I've met many people, believers and unbelievers, who still do. *Do you?* We all need to look at this question. Even if your answer is no, you may be worshiping it in ways you don't understand.

If you do not believe in God, I think my point can still be received, because it is against our very nature to live from a place of deviance, violence, fear, shame, or confusion. Every person struggling with incorrect understandings of sex and sexuality in some way experiences one, or all, of the emotions above. Period.

We are made for sex. At the biological level, it is the mechanism for the reproduction of our species. But we are also made for the mental, emotional, and physical connection that sex creates.

You need only look at the plethora of sexual confusion and deviation to know someone, somewhere, sold us the wrong bill of goods. We have misunderstood something about ourselves. We have disconnected from some things we should be deeply connected to. Unrestrained pursuit of selfish sexual pleasure should not be the focus of nearly everything we do. Yet it is.

The Solution: In a Nutshell

Sex is about more than feeling good in a moment. It is important for our emotional and spiritual development. Experiencing sex rightly offers you true, lasting freedom. This freedom comes through the pursuit of purity in each season of life.

Purity applies to the way we think, the way we feel, and the way we live. While sex is a physical act that elicits visceral feelings and visceral emotions, purity is something that is rational, and we only understand that when we commit to its power. It requires a choice, and that choice brings freedom—from confusion, battles with self-esteem, and yearning for anything outside of yourself.

When I finally experienced what a life of choosing purity of mind, body, and soul really was, I became the most confident and powerful I have ever been in my life. I am more desirable than

I have ever been or felt, and most importantly, I am desirable to me. I like myself. You should like yourself too!

As you read these pages, you will come to understand all that you might be losing and all that you will gain from a life lived with purity. Many folks in the Church have called for purity in the past. But theirs is an archaic, old conversation that seems uncool, unhip, and outdated. Many have spoken of purity revolutions and purity culture but without any real compassion, understanding, or sympathy for those who don't get what they're talking about, don't believe what they're talking about, and don't understand *why* we should give up something so great as sex without commitment.

Most people don't understand why swiping *left* on today's culture of sex without marriage, and sex without even love, is actually a powerful place of freedom we can arrive at that gives us *everything* we want. Your "no" until the right time provides more freedom for you than your "yes" said over and over and over again.

Embracing the power of your no to all the cultural chaos surrounding sex and sexuality will give you a proper understanding of sex and its place in your life and relationships. I hope to help you redirect the sinking Titanic you may have been on for some time now and deliver you safely to the shores of a new way of thinking and living!

Whatever stage of life or season you are in, it is not too late to turn the ship around and go in a different direction. It is not too late to understand and embrace healthy sexuality and sacred sex.

By now you may be asking yourself if this book is really for you. Well, that depends! Are you ever utterly shocked or even mildly weirded out at the various displays of sexual behavior all around you? Do you ever experience confusion, doubt, or insecurity about sex? Do you find that you have nobody to really talk to about sex and sexuality and how they relate to your identity? Do you ever feel confused about your own sexuality or that of someone else? Has your own behavior ever surprised or even shocked you concerning sex, sexuality, or the notion of living in a way that is not in line with what you intuitively know is right? Do you often feel undesirable? Do you equate someone being sexually attracted to you with truly desiring *you*? Do you feel unseen and misunderstood by the person you are currently having sex with? Do you believe you will never find your "soul mate," if that even exists at all? Do you feel that your sex life will never be satisfying? Do you think you have intimacy issues, trust issues, or any other issue dealing with the opposite sex?

Do you find yourself thinking about your "glory days" of sexual behavior when sex perhaps seemed better? Do you long to live free from guilt about sex? Do you feel OK having sex with anyone of any gender? Do you feel your marriage is lacking in any real depth or excitement sexually? Do you have a hard time desiring your spouse? Is there a feeling of shame or awkwardness that you experience after sex—even though you are married?

Let me boil it all down to one all-encompassing question: *Are you using sex to get love—or love to get sex?*

If the answer is *yes* to any of the above, then what you are about to read should create a revolution inside of you that you have no choice but to confront! If you take this journey toward this new revolution with me, you will find that truth is so rooted in common sense that the guarantee of victory exists—whether you are a Christian or not.

On this journey, what I do not want to do is preach to the choir only. I am writing this book to my Christian and my non-Christian brothers and sisters to embrace. I am an evangelist at heart. But I am as clear about my call to wake up the Church as I am about our shared call to reach those we see as lost outside of it.

I say without doubt that there is one bridge that must be built for you to walk across to achieve the victory you want. I am trying to build that bridge with my very life. It may begin in our secular world, where there are no rules or limits, but it most certainly ends in a world where your victory is found through surrender to Jesus—a very revolutionary guy indeed.

This book is for all people. Just as Jesus is for all people.

Inside these pages it will become very clear that I am quite bold and uncompromised concerning Jesus and the inerrant Word of God, just as I am bold concerning politics and everything else in this world of ours. Love is bold. And it is often confrontational because, for me, Truth is important, people are important, and purity is important.

While I speak much of purity and a purity revolution, it is purposely not in my book title at all. Why? Because this isn't a watered-down version of a Christian book on *no sex before marriage*. This is a book that shows you unequivocally that the sexual freedom you may *think* you have is not freedom at all.

The promise of gaining sexual freedom is what everyone wants. Whether secular or religious, for right or wrong reasons, everyone wants clarity about sex and sexuality. While abstinence is the key to that, it's not the only key, nor is impure sex the only impurity you should be avoiding. Purity and impurity exist on many levels. They are rooted in the subconscious, and they flow into the conscious world we live in.

So what do you do right now?

You must do what I have known for years now. You must revolt. You must consider that a revolution in thought is required.

It is long past time for a new way of thinking. It is time to talk about it in a real way, argue about it, and get it together. The sexual revolution sold us a glamorous lie. The feminist movement cemented more untruths than truths. Both are failed experiments at best. The experiment was on us all, and we bear the wounds of its failures. The only revolution that will save us now is one that returns us to our God-given identity which was created for purity in our minds, our bodies, and our souls.

CHAPTER 1

UNVEILING THE PAST

The History of Sex in the World

L et's begin by taking a broad and general look back.

The history of sex in the world is as long and complex as the history of mankind's relationship to God.

From the beginning of time, society revolved around men serving their God and living to please their God. God had rules for man's protection, and man followed the rules. Kings established rules and answered to God for those rules. Godly order brought peace and stability. The opposite was chaos—and nobody benefits when chaos reigns.

In Christian theology, God created man, Adam. He recognized that man, Adam, needed a partner. So He created Eve. When they walked with God and talked with God in the Garden of Eden, they had no shame, they had no confusion, and they lived in perfect peace. It wasn't until they rejected God's plan for them that they experienced utter chaos. Through that rebellious mistake they made, nobody has benefited since.

The Greeks and Egyptians left the serving of One God and had multiple gods that they served. In fact, the "gods" were created as justifications for how man really *wanted* to live. There was a god for every lust of the flesh and a god for every desire. This shifting of focus to self-rule and self-pleasure is likely why the Greeks and the Romans had no issues with very open behaviors sexually—like having orgies. Sex was not at all sacred. It was not at all reserved for a man and a woman made in the image of God as monogamous partners.

Sexuality was completely twisted to whatever men could imagine to please themselves, because pleasing God was not their concern. They sought to pleasure themselves, so they had a god associated with each pleasure they desired—to make it all right, so to speak.

There was Bacchus, the Roman god of wine and pleasure. Also called Dionysus by the Greeks, he was the Greek god of fertility.

Eros, also called Cupid by the Romans, was the Greek god of love, passion, and desire. You know the story; Cupid would shoot an arrow at your heart and bring confusion and crazy, irrepressible feelings.

Hedone, the daughter of Eros, was the goddess of sensual pleasure and enjoyment. There was even a god of both genders who was portrayed in Greco Roman art as a female with male genitals. This symbol of twisted sexual androgyny was named Hermaphroditus and was believed to be the child of Aphrodite and Hermes (Venus and Mercury).

In the ancient world of the Greeks and Romans, gods and goddesses existed solely for their individual and fleshly pursuits.

Exalted in an elegant and noble way, these gods stood as the justi-fication for exalting the base, demeaning, and immoral acts com-mitted by the elites who created them.

Humans, without God for a conscience and if left to them-selves, will pursue their own individual desires to the exclusion of anyone and anything else. This way of thinking and living was certainly opposite from the monolithic God-centered societies that once existed in the beginning of the world.

With the Greek philosophers came the shift toward reasoning and debating with each other about how to live. The focus shifted from serving gods to serving self even further. In fact, they went further and further away from needing to justify having gods at all. Gods became less godlike, and man became more of a god *himself*.

Plato's teacher Socrates would solidify not just a new way of thinking and reasoning, but a new way of governing. Plato's *Republic* was established alongside the gods, but eventually the gods weren't even necessary. This was the logical next shift further into the abyss. Men became their own voices of reason, serving nothing higher than themselves. This brought the gods down—and elevated man.

Government eventually shifted to man-centered democracies and congresses like what we have established around the world today. When you see a debate in our US Congress, it is a form of the system established by the philosophers. Men argue their own points of view, often based on nothing more than what they *feel* or *desire* to be true or correct.

Once man became the god of himself, we became ripe for any type of revolution or movement that seemed acceptable to a majority of men—or a vocal minority of men who were more powerful than the majority.

Usually, in this new governmental thinking, when things seemed unfair, men could revolt and do the things they reasoned to be better for themselves and the life they wanted. They formed new governments or societies—like the United States of America.

In America, we saw taxation without representation as wrong, and rightly so. So, we sought to form a new government in a new land. While God is discussed all throughout the Constitution and the Declaration of Independence, you must understand that the governmental system underneath was still built on the foundations provided by the Greek philosophers, Plato's *Republic*, and the Roman Senate. Men created their own ideas for government.

In our specific American case we prayed for guidance, evidencing a belief in a single God, just like in the beginning of our world history, but we were still involved in crafting and making decisions ourselves. For example, the issue of slavery is a battle we chose at the outset of our nation to lose in order to win the war over freedom from an oppressive king.

Slavery was a system America inherited from England. It was something many of the Founders knew was wrong, yet based on the economics of slavery, some men simply saw no way out.

Some men, however, saw it as a moral choice and a matter of doing the right thing. But ultimately, those men who wanted slavery would be allowed to win for a time in order to start the new Republic.

In short, now that men could reason amongst themselves by virtue of where the world had evolved—or devolved—slavery was accepted until it wasn't. Many things have been wrongly accepted throughout history because we choose to placate men's opinions and lose battles to win wars. In human thinking, on any issue, we should only see one war—the war between what God says is right and what God says is wrong. If He is sovereign and on a throne above all, then our focus would be on serving Him and never ourselves. However, we've allowed the mixing in of our will with our service to God.

The next step in this evolution led us to a newly formed America in which mixed foundations existed. Foundations of a monolithic God-centered society coexist today with a Greek and Roman flesh-centered DNA. If everything flows from this unstable spiritual foundation in which the gods, or God, are no longer above us, but we are in fact equal to them or can be a god ourselves, then no wonder we were ripe for two specific movements that celebrated a return to Greco-Roman orgies with women seen as whores or a Madonna, and men able to do whatever they want to please their fleshly desires.

The Decline into the Unsacred: The Movements That Shaped Us All

In the intricate tapestry of American history, the subject of sex has woven a complex and compelling narrative. From the Greeks and Romans to the feminist movement to the Sexual Revolution to #MeToo and #Time'sUp, society has experienced profound shifts in attitudes and behaviors surrounding human sexuality. The seismic and continual shifting is evidence of a faulty foundation. Something's just not solid. We all know it.

I believe the only way we can realize the drastic need we all have for a final change is to understand the historical context of these movements, examining their impact and the repercussions that have unfolded over time. By exploring these events, we gain a deeper understanding of how society has changed—and why we need to seek out purity for our lives, more so today than ever before.

In this quest for understanding the sacredness of sex, it is *essential* to understand that somewhere along the way sex became devalued. How is something that was created to be *sacred* used so *unsacredly*? The reasons are clearly found in our history concerning sex.

Yet, you might say, there is some good in these movements. Sure, there is. But if the founders of these movements had good intentions—then what went wrong? As we explore this journey through time, contemplate the consequences of these movements in your life—and especially in the lives of women.

Remarkable shifts occurred in American society during the feminist movement and the Sexual Revolution. These transformative periods have given us insights into the impact they had on women and their relationship with sex. I believe that the more you understand about the history of sex in America, the more you will opt in on a new revolution. The more you understand what went wrong historically, the more you will understand the urgency of fully exploring the notion of returning to traditional Judeo-Christian values as a pathway to walking in your identity, calling, and purpose.

The feminist movement and the sexual revolution were once referred to collectively as a major challenging of the status quo. Yet we were willing to accept that challenge because we thought things could be made better for men and for women. We saw problems, and we chose to use our freedoms to solve those problems. Sadly, we chose wrong. Inadvertently, we chose bondage—just as Adam and Eve did, when they were left understanding that their nakedness, in a moment of choosing flesh, had covered them in shame.

My question for you right now in this book is simple: Will you fight the system, go against your peers, rise up, use your voice, your vote, and your dollars to change things that will no doubt destroy us if we don't change them now?

Will you risk being canceled and seen as uncool to walk in ultimate coolness and complete freedom?

Will you find and embrace your true identity and choose to help others do the same—especially those younger than you?

Will you consider a new challenge to make things right?

Challenging the Status Quo: The Feminist Movement

While I have seen and lived through the dire consequences of the feminist movement, let me try to be unbiased in explaining its intentions.

The feminist movement of the late nineteenth and early twentieth centuries ignited a fire of change that reverberated across American society. Driven by seeking equality and freedom from traditional gender roles, suffragettes fought tirelessly for women's right to vote, marking a significant milestone in the struggle for gender parity. As the movement progressed, it broadened its scope to include reproductive rights and sexual liberation.

This movement claimed to *liberate* women from oppressive gender norms and *empower* them to embrace their own desires. Everything became measured by this question: *"If men can do it, why can't we?"* Yes, women wanted equal pay, but they also wanted more than marriage and sex within its usual confines. Nobody really considered that *we* shouldn't be doing everything *men* can do *because* we are *women!*

The feminist movement caused a profound shift in the social fabric of America by empowering women to pursue education, careers, and greater independence. This wasn't a bad thing and was certainly a worthy goal on the surface. But there was so much more to consider than this surface freedom.

As it collided with sexual freedom, the fabric of our society began to corrode. Perhaps historically these movements were spurred on by well-meaning people with good intentions. But perhaps there were some with bad intentions who simply saw women's perceived bondage to traditional values as a means to an end—something to be manipulated.

Sadly, it is debatable whether the *intentions* of this movement were noble. And, whether good or bad, the consequences have emerged gradually into what we now see today as disastrous.

While the feminist movement has undeniably achieved some advancements in women's rights and opportunities, you simply have to hear the critics accounting for the negative consequences that the movement has had to understand why many secular feminists around the world, like Louise Perry in her book *The Case against the Sexual Revolution*, think that both the feminist movement and the concurrent sexual revolution completely failed.

First, we have had a fragmentation of our traditional family structures. By challenging traditional gender roles and prioritizing individual fulfillment, the fulfillment found in family and in our individual roles as mothers and fathers have broken. This has led to a decline in the importance placed on marriage and commitment, impacting the stability of families and creating challenges for women and children—especially children.

Critics contend that the false glamorization of women being able to balance both careers and family responsibilities has resulted in increased emotional stress and depression when you realize that you cannot have it *all* if you want to do any of it *well*.

In a powerful expose in *The Atlantic* written by Anne-Marie Slaughter, the first woman director of policy planning at the State Department who worked for two years in Washington with Hillary Clinton and her chief of staff, Cheryl Mills, wrote that the lie that women can have it all and do it all well is one she could no longer help perpetrate. "I am hardly alone in this realization."[1] Slaughter writes, "Michèle Flournoy stepped down after three years as undersecretary of defense for policy, the third-highest job in the department, to spend more time at home with her three children, two of whom are teenagers. Karen Hughes left her position as the counselor to President George W. Bush after a year and a half in Washington to go home to Texas for the sake of her family. Mary Matalin, who spent two years as an assistant to Bush and the counselor to Vice President Dick Cheney stepped down to spend more time with her daughters."[2]

Slaughter added, "Women of my generation have clung to the feminist credo we were raised with, even as our ranks have been steadily thinned by unresolvable tensions between family and career, because we are determined not to drop the flag for the next generation. But when many members of the younger generation have stopped listening, on the grounds that glibly repeating 'you can have it all' is simply airbrushing reality, it is time to talk."[3]

And talk we must. The expectation to excel in all areas of life has created a sense of guilt, burnout, and the overwhelming feeling of being *overwhelmed*. Especially when this lie is packaged beautifully on magazine covers—for *single* women to buy into.

As a single mother, I believed this lie for years. I placed my hopes in it after finding myself a single mom who still wanted a career in Hollywood. It was enough to see other actresses and TV personalities I admired "having it all" to believe the lie that I could too. These girls were smiling on the cover of *People Magazine*, holding their babies, and dating the hot new "guy," while looking very much like they were "having it all." We could all achieve it if they could. Couldn't we?

As my career grew and I started to get to know some of these famous poster girls for the "you can have it all club," I realized many were stressed and unhappy.

The couple other Christian women I knew in Hollywood lived as secularly as I did back then, and in hindsight, we simply put Jesus on the list of everything else we could have when "having it all." In reality, Jesus gets less than anything or anybody in the "having it all" lie.

Basically, at a certain point I realized that everything the lie sold me was against everything else that I considered truth. As if on par with the truth, the selfish desire for love, career, and sex is clearly what wins out.

In all our adult chaos, I met very, very few of the children of my famous friends who felt as if they had solid, stable families to lean on mentally and emotionally. I am certain I wasn't the rock of stability mentally and emotionally through many of my years as a young mother to my son.

The feminist movement aimed to combat the objectification of women. But critics argue that the emphasis on sexual liberation and the commodification of the female body, which emerged during and after the sexual revolution, have contributed to the continued objectification of women in society. In short, women are more objectified than ever.

I consider myself a true and enlightened feminist in the godly sense of the word, meaning that I want women's empowerment to come from equal pay, honor for how we are created, respect for our intellect, and true confidence in our abilities—beyond our body parts. I am deeply saddened for my poor little sisters who are being used up by a game called female self-empowerment that is not real. It is female self-abuse created by agendas that serve the men who abuse them.

Music also freely glamorizes the abuse of women in every song about "big butts" to Cardi B's "WAP." Yet, nobody dares to criticize that women's rights are being trampled on by these songs every time they're played. Most don't want to be considered *uncool* or worse, *old*. But why is nobody questioning that perhaps the two main movements of our female sexual history are perhaps uncool, old, and totally in need of revision after years and years of proven failure?

The question of whether these movements protect women today can be complex and subjective, absent Jesus's opinion. But would we really need "reproductive rights"—that is, abortion, let's call it what it is—if we were committed to living in monogamous unions in which we were loved and valued?

Would the words "women's rights" even be necessary if we were all treated kindly, loved sincerely, and respected equally?

And what gender stereotypes would we need to challenge if we all respected and accepted that we are in fact created differently from birth with amazingly different roles on earth?

What is empowering is that our roles are mutually non-exclusive and interdependent. We need each other for the whole thing to work. Therefore, we are very, very, equal.

I have been asked recently, *"What about our objectification—the pressure to behave as men sexually, and the full court press to be silent when men say they are us—is evidence of equality today?"*

Well, that's an easy question to answer. None of it evidences our equality. It simply underscores our *inequality*. All of this has allowed society to degrade and demean us. And when a society degrades women and sees them as merely sex objects and body parts—even with their willing participation—we clearly put them at risk of all types of violence and abuse.

Women must value themselves and our hard-won freedoms as much more than just the freedom to have sex like men. We are *not* men, so having sex like men is an impossibility—and it always will be.

Ladies, there is a double standard! Men and women cannot have or view sex and sexuality in the same way. God didn't make us the same. When it comes to unsacred sex, there is nothing wrong with tapping out. *Do we really want this freedom anyway?* To act against ourselves mentally, physically, emotionally, and spiritually?

It's bad enough that men are conditioned by society to connect their masculinity to their sexual prowess. But women will never find status, or real rewards, in being defined by their sexual prowess or promiscuity. Yet in the name of equality, we have gone down with the Titanic and chosen to call it empowerment. So have many of the men. It just plays itself out differently.

For men, there is a sadness I see in needing to play a game to be perceived as macho or masculine. There is also a rage and an anger I see. The confusion created in the souls of young boys and men is just as real as that created in the souls of women.

The impurity of the feminist movement destroyed a man's identity as hunter, provider, protector, and father. It emasculated him year after year and continues to emasculate him today. This movement has reduced men to far less than what God created them to be, and we as women should apologize for what we've allowed to become of our feminine "equality."

With the loaded gun in our hands, today females are even losing their protections under Title IX because of the misapplication of the trans movement to it. Title IX was created to benefit and protect *women* and *girls* from discrimination against them, especially in sports.

Title IX requires schools and colleges that receive federal funds to give women and girls an equal chance to play sports and to treat men and women equally when it comes to athletic scholarships and other benefits like equipment, coaching, and facilities. It inherently acknowledges that women and men are *different* by insisting on separate but equal facilities available to them on every level.

Specifically enacted to protect girls in sports, we now see that new challenges and inequalities persist. Men who *feel* as if they are women want protection under laws designed to protect us from them, men. The fact that some men's gender dysphoria or identity confusion interferes with our rights must be considered.

If girls are to blossom with self-esteem and confidence into the women they were created to be, then telling them that men can become women is wrong. It is also wrong to do so while allowing these same men to compete against them, all while silencing the truth that men are stronger than they are physically. It's almost shocking that an advanced nation would play this absurd mind game with itself. Gender dysphoria should never dismantle the protections of a protected class by those whom they are protected from.

When you consider the above transgender dilemma, you quickly see that the feminist movement overlooked the beauty of *reality* and *why* the status quo became the *status quo*. Women as real women are important. We carry the eggs of the future in our *wombs*. Men as real men are also important. They plant the seed. The beauty is that we are interdependent. We work together—when we work together. *Nothing* can ever change that. In our quest to be open to working together on this issue, let's remember not be so open that our brains fall out of our heads!

Feminism today is not just the failed experiment it is now being called, but one with radical consequences. We are not empowered. We are not happy. We are not free. We are sexualized, beaten into submission as man-pleasers—more than ever before in history.

Young girls alter their bodies, their faces, and their hearts and souls to achieve a state they call female empowerment. What is empowering about being in a world in which you are essentially told to change everything about yourself to be accepted? What is empowering about being in a world where the same men you have sex with tell you that they too can *be you*?

Are we not more special than this?

The Sexual Revolution: The Freedom to Be in Bondage

Liberation or licentiousness? That is the question!

Building upon the shaky foundation being laid by the feminist movement and somewhat paralleling it, the 1960s also witnessed the dawn of the sexual revolution. Throughout the 1960s and 1970s, this cultural upheaval further challenged traditional notions of sexuality, sparking a wave of sexual openness and exploration, advocating for a more permissive attitude towards sexual expression. Free love, casual relationships, and the normalization of premarital sex became the prevailing ideologies.

This era also witnessed a rebellion against what it called conservative sexual norms. The sexual revolution instead advocated for sexual freedom, contraception, and the acceptance of diverse sexual orientations.

The contraceptive pill's introduction in 1960 revolutionized women's ability to control their reproductive choices, giving rise to a newfound sense of autonomy—albeit a terrifying one. It opened Pandora's box, so to speak, and sadly, without a need to be responsible, boundaries dissolved. As do millions of children yearly through abortion.

There was an increased acceptance of premarital sex and a greater emphasis on personal freedom and individual expression in matters of sex and sexuality. The consequences of this sexual liberation started to unfold, altering the fabric of relationships and individual well-being forever. And it has been downhill ever since.

Our quick return to the self-pleasure, self-ruling, hedonistic behaviors of the Greeks and Romans has deteriorated into chaos as surely as it did for them. Many have made pleasing the flesh their idol. And sacrificing caution, feelings, and even unborn babies is of no consequence to those who place no value on purity.

I believe that absent a resurgence of good old-fashioned purity and Judeo-Christian values, we will destroy ourselves with our sexual freedoms, our sexual confusion, and our sexual blindness.

The sexual revolution has awakened our lust, our greed, and our selfishness on every level. Relationships today don't have a need to mirror God's original intentions because the sexual revolution tore into the fabric of anything *God* wanted and made it about what *we want*. Mostly folks seem to want sex. In any form. And to make matters worse, you can have what you want without the consequences designed for sex by God—children, responsibility, commitment, and intimacy.

#MeToo #Time'sUp: The Almost Revolution

Then came hope.

Movements like #MeToo and #Time'sUp saw women reclaim their sexual power by saying, "STOP! You are wrong for making me feel diminished sexually." Suddenly, as history wound its way from ancient history to present history, women began to get upset and vocal about what they were receiving, and not receiving, in their exchanges with men. They gathered together to declare, "We will not take the unwanted abuses and assaults any longer."

Sadly, these movements stopped short of reclaiming what sex and sexuality really should be about! And they definitely did not explain *why* women have been abused, pimped, and marginalized so many times by the greatest figureheads in Hollywood and captains of industry. Yes, some men are falling to court cases for abuse claims—even claims of abuses that occurred twenty years prior—but nobody is looking at or discussing the why of it all. We should not be here. We should have progressed so much further if the feminist revolution and the sexual revolution really were the answer to empowering women.

I remember sitting with my girlfriend Debra, a powerhouse of beauty and intellect, at her home in Cannes one summer. #MeToo and #Time'sUp were breaking movements, and accusations of abuses by powerful men were emerging all over the globe. She and I discussed the importance of women with podiums speaking up to help protect those women without podiums, platforms, and positions.

I really thought the world would finally change. I saw hope that there would be some realization that sex *is* sacred. I thought the chaos of the charges being claimed by famous and powerful women around the globe would bring clarity to a world of historic confusion—and give a voice to the poor and needy women who have no voice or high-priced lawyer to defend them.

But sadly, neither #MeToo nor #Time'sUp did anything to make sexuality less confusing to anyone. Many men still don't really know what the boundaries are and where the lines exist between compliment and harassment. And #MeToo still does nothing to empower women in general.

Worse still, as the bright lights of celebrity cases and household names faded, giving way to abuses against normal women—whom the world cares nothing about—we saw that the protections that were so important when it came to famous Hollywood actresses weren't really that important at all. Minus a Harvey Weinstein and a list of globally known starlets, nobody cares.

So day after day I continue to see precious young girls broken by unmet expectations as they continue to give their bodies away, hoping to gain *something*. Hoping to prove they are worth it—to prove to a guy who rejected them that they are valuable.

#Time'sUp and #MeToo owed more to the millions of children sexually abused and trafficked around the world today than it has ever acknowledged. It owed more to every nameless, faceless woman and man who needed their voices to fight for them too. Yet sadly, the inequity of reality for men and women who've been marginalized by their color or social status still exists. Even in movements designed to protect us, we discover that the "us" protected is *not* all of us.

Worse still, throughout history, all these movements do little if anything for any of us if we continue to abuse ourselves by participating in a game that has a bar so low you must stoop to now get under it.

How do we participate, you ask?

Have you ever looked at the beautiful young girls who model for the clothing brand PrettyLittleThings? Some make money. Some have millions of followers. But none own the swimsuits and clothing they are selling. And when they are too old to play this game, what happens to them? Nobody cares.

Well, I do. I care. I look at them and see myself as a young twenty-something-year-old girl serving sexy photos and a smile to be approved and get work. These girls, like I did, have dreams. And without any system of behavior in place to guide and nurture them, they get used, abused, and tossed aside. Yet we all willingly walk toward the slaughter of our dreams like lambs. Simply because we have a little girl fantasy of success in Hollywood, we are not weaker animals to be preyed upon by even weaker men.

This shouldn't happen in America, where we claim to have fought for women's rights! But what are *our rights*, I ask myself as I survey today's landscape? From what I see, it appears we have simply settled for—or been relegated to—only the right to present ourselves like sex objects for male gratification.

What difference does #MeToo or #Time'sUp make when we invite predators into our souls with our own behavior by participating in a game the predators created for us to deceive ourselves in? The damage of all this to our souls and to our society is monumental. And it's time for monumental change.

CHAPTER 2

THE DAMAGED SELF

The Aftermath

A re we damaged by these prior revolutions and movements? Yes. In every way.

The numerous emotional impacts include detachment from each other and a decline in overall relationship satisfaction for all of us. Many women—and men—know the pain of not receiving a call the next day and feeling like the other person is playing games with you. Or worse, that the other person is just not that into you *after* sleeping with you. How about that for emotional damage? Once you've become one through sex with someone, being treated as a separate entity is a shock to the system. It makes me cry over how it makes all girls cry.

All girls are wired to be treated as princesses and queens. We are not wired to be taken and tossed aside like trash. Nobody is. But something about the psyche of women causes us to harden in ways that are against our nature in response to the casual way we allow ourselves to be treated today.

With the sexual freedom these movements have given us, the perception of sex has undergone a very unsacred transformation in the aftermath. Most of us start relationships by trying to prove our love too quickly with sex. But what we are actually proving is our lust.

Love takes time and testing through experiences and commitment to grow. No doubt many women hope and yearn for it to grow and replace the number of dysfunctional unions they have allowed for themselves. Commitment is the safe zone for sex— and sex outside of that zone is unsafe.

Even the rise in more dating shows centered around making a "connection" is proof of our actual desire to connect on a deeper level than merely having sex with each other—even if we won't admit it.

The media have played a significant role in affirming everything about the sexual revolution by perpetuating completely unrealistic standards of beauty, sex, and sexuality. Thanks to the media, we often face pressure to conform to narrow ideals, leading to increased objectification and diminished self-worth. How can a beautiful girl compete with every other flavor of beautiful girl? How can a sexy girl be sexier than a porn star—if sex is seen through the eyes of a guy who watches and enjoys pornography?

What must you do to compete with everything else that exists for you to compete with?

In the aftermath of the sexual revolution, the emphasis on external appearances overshadowed the recognition of inner qualities and personal accomplishments. That feeling of being unseen by someone you are having sex with, who should see you most clearly, is a tragedy many of us have experienced.

But when you are in competition mode with every other person of your sex, by virtue of not being seen for the special and unique prize that you are, you don't even recognize with adequate weight your own inner qualities or personal accomplishments.

Casual sex has become rampant, and while the emphasis on finding a real emotional connection has diminished, the demand for a fantasy connection has increased to epic proportions.

Just look at the Netflix show *Too Hot to Handle*, in which a group of young people get to an island and discover they *can't* have sex. They are sadly devastated and struggle episode after episode not to lose all the money they can win if they can simply *not* engage in sex—which they all went there excited to casually engage in.

As reported by The Ringer, "The show tells us that in these 10 islanders, it has found the world's "hottest, horniest, commitment-phobic swipesters," and those swipesters would seem to agree quite proudly with this assessment."[1] They all believed they were headed for a "hedonistic" vacation. "The revelation is met with shrieks, cursing, wailing, and horror."[2]

"Sex, they tell us—having it, mostly, but also their ability to have it most any time with a great many readily obliging some-ones, found at bars and libraries and churches and also, in one case, the hotel the very night before taping—is a vital part of their identities," the report continued. "One contestant compares the ban to learning that her mother has died. 'What I'm most proud of is my penis,' says another, by way of introduction."[3]

You get the point. Netflix's show is a celebration of the height—or really the low—of the sexual revolution if you watch even five minutes.

The unique goal of the show, on the other hand, is to get the contestants to open up and have deeper and more meaningful *connections*. The producers are trying to teach them that they need more than just sex. They need meaningful connections.

I agree with their goal, though the word "connection" is overused and misunderstood on all these dating shows from *The Bachelor* to *Love Island*. The "connection" these young men and women are looking for is a sexual one. As a result, the goal of intimacy and meaningful relationships is almost always overshadowed by physical gratification and the pursuit of immediate pleasure. These shows represent the aftermath of both revolutions at work!

The mental confusion between what is desired by the flesh and what is needed by the soul sets the stage for all of us to watch the worst of where we are culturally.

While these shows are a mockery, you'll discover that the tears shed *always* evidence a desire for real and committed connections. Once the façade of sexually charged behavioral walls are taken down, what we find is not surprising: battered, broken, misguided little children trying to fit into a mold none of us was born to fit into. A mold that tells us we don't need what we truly need. A mold that feeds us poison and calls it our empowered choice to drink it. A mold that tells us what sexual freedom is when it's really showing us what sexual bondage looks like.

As societal norms have shifted into the lies promised by these sexual revolutions, the idea of sex and sexuality detached from emotional and relational commitment is terrifying. Women were once revered as nurturers and pillars of stability. We were the fabric of the home and of family life. Even today, while dad may make a baby with mom, it's always mama's baby and papa's maybe in a society free of commitment. Just ask any Kardashian.

These Kardashian girls are a textbook study in the history of the "free sex, empowered feminist, mental madness" that leaves us worse off than before. It is no wonder they *behave* as they do. Their *behavior* is a direct response to their acceptance of the culture surrounding them. Do you need to ask which came first—the chicken or the egg?

They, like you, no longer live in a world where when a boy gets a girl pregnant, he feels pressured by society, his family, and himself to marry her and make an "honest" woman out of her.

Instead, the boy splits, not having had a deep connection or desire for commitment in the first place. The girl is left holding the bag—or baby—while trying to salvage her dignity. Today, women have created a false way to scrape together a modicum of self-respect because society has made a place for the term "baby-mama" to mean something more than it really is—just a woman who has had a baby out of wedlock for a guy who didn't marry her.

The damage is so evident. The aftermath of what we called a revolution, and a movement of female empowerment, more resembles the toxic waste of Chernobyl. It is both invisibly and visibly destroying people.

All women—no matter how successful, how famous, how important, how beautiful, or how smart they are—have found themselves navigating a world that promotes instant gratification and temporary connections. Period. It's like you know you are special, yet you just can't make him treat you that way!

Among the most notable changes in the aftermath of our sexual history, according to Child Trends, is the "increase in . . . the percentage of all children born to unmarried parents. Recent estimates show that about 40 percent of births in the United States occur outside of marriage, up from 28 percent in 1990 (Child

Trends, 2016). This increase is consistent with changes in non-marital childbearing seen worldwide (Chamie, 2017)."[4]

Intimacy and connection should be precursors to commitment. Both are required for lasting relationships, healthy connections, and certainly for raising children. Yet our sexual history as a nation has eliminated the need for intimacy, connection—or even children. So, when a girl chooses to play the game, the kids are hers to deal with alone, much to the detriment of the poor kids born into the dysfunction of it all.

The Emotional Aftermath: Mentally Broken

Women are broken. Men are broken. Children are broken. Broken people break others as the cycle of our historical rebellion against what is pure and good continues. Unless we choose to wake up, the worst emotional brokenness we will experience in the aftermath of all our history is complete numbness to the "truth" in the obvious face of right and wrong.

When you look at pop culture, our national brokenness is glamorized by it, so it's not seen clearly for the damage it's doing. The culture of lies we live in keeps us blind to the truth by glamorizing the cultural agenda and using people who are broken and numb to "truth" themselves as its agents.

It's especially glamorized by the many celebrities who jump from relationship to relationship with marriages that rarely—if ever—last. Purity is not celebrated in Hollywood at all, because Hollywood is just people broken by the aftermath of the culture that has broken all of us. So many of the celebrities I've known have a hard time creating successful marriages because they engage in so much that is outside of what we are created for, simply by virtue of their jobs as actors.

As actors they are asked to live life skilled in selling whatever behaviors, impure or not, are glamorized by the TV shows and movies they act in. It's difficult to live a normal life when so much of the abnormal is not just available to you but expected of you.

To make matters more complicated, fame, wealth, or status often puts people in a false safety zone in which, no matter what they do, because other people desire to be part of their world, they never deal honestly with the truth that they may be part of selling lies that damage millions of people. Unplugging while you're a relevant part of "The Matrix," as most celebrities are, is nearly impossible. There is money, position, status, and "fun" on the inside of the culture of lies—even if your insides are dying because the blue pill is making you sick. (For those who don't understand my constant reference to this box-office award-winning film and cultural phenomenon, let me explain. *The Matrix* movie follows a character played by Keanu Reeves as he chooses to unplug from a system of lies and embrace truth by taking a red pill—versus the blue pill which will return him to his former life of unknowing bliss.)

Worse still, being *seen* by millions—and unseen by anyone in particular—often caused me when I became famous to experience a terrible state of loneliness. I had people's attention, but I didn't have deep commitment from them. These things are different. One heals you. The other can further wound you.

Being wanted for money or power or access is as bad as being wanted simply for sex. With all of that combined, it can be a lonely, inauthentic, and traumatizing existence. It is no wonder to me why we see famous people commit suicide. They are the objects of sexual lust and multiple levels of desire who often live isolated from authentic connections with people who want them for who they are, and not who their images say they are.

Impurity has crept so far into the psyche of our culture that our souls are literally diseased. When impurity plagues your soul, you are dead even while alive. Impurity has broken all of our hearts at one time or another, and the emotional aftermath of an "anything goes" culture has destroyed our understanding of what is truly right and wrong for our human condition to flourish healthily and happily.

It isn't difficult to see the connection between all of this mental anguish and confusion and the lost hope of all of these movements. Our essential human experience of love and safety and deep lasting connection to each other, much less to one significant person, has been destroyed by our rebellion against the safeguards provided by purity in the mind, body, and soul as a way of life.

Today, you can connect with more people than ever before for your dopamine hit, but we have no real connection in the isolation of our world. Loneliness and depression have become the legacy of our recent generations. In fact, many people who experience depression do so because of loneliness as a major contributing factor, according to a study from the National Library of Medicine.[5] It should be clear that loneliness is spreading like wildfire because we've been told that we can become one with others sexually while never becoming one emotionally.

We can hide behind our computer screens and engage in sexual foreplay and all manner of sexual perversion while never really revealing who we are to the person we may be engaging with. Isolated in a world of despair about your behavior—as most people become when they find themselves as another nameless, faceless, victim of our sexually free culture—you end up mentally twisted into a million lonely, depressed pieces.

Our perceived sexual freedom has enslaved us to everything that is against God, which in turn actually puts us in mental bondage. When our actions don't line up with what we inherently know is true, we experience feelings of separation from all that keeps us safe. While only His purity can set us free, there is a total misunderstanding of purity and outright backlash to the purity culture of the past. More on this later. But suffice it to say, our *questioning* of morality and monogamy has made morality and monogamy things of the past. Yet they are now, more than ever, the things we need most.

The Matrix of lies that culture has glamorized is not selling morality, monogamy, or purity at all. And our way proves itself wrong *again*. God's way proves itself right *again*. Nobody exemplifies morality and monogamy like our risen Savior. The incongruence and instability many of you may feel in terms of life today is your proof that building your life on shaky ground is leaving you emotionally unwell.

When it comes to sex and sexuality, millions of people today appear to be more in *bondage* than they appear to be in *freedom*. In questioning whether sex is sacred, while elevating our own appetites above God's plan for us, we have made sex into nothing, and in the process, we have made sexuality confusing.

Yes, confusing. In the search for sexual identity, just think about the utter absurdity of pronouns. Only in the aftermath of the total destruction of the purity of sex and sexuality could we entertain calling people "gender fluid" and assigning "pronouns" as if they change the *facts* of who you were born to be.

Sexuality simply cannot be reduced to absurd labels applied to people confused about why their natural gender cannot be changed, while demanding that we recognize them in their mental delusion as normal. As if the world is blind, our history has led us to a place of total darkness and asks that we call it light. We use terms like "woke" for "asleep at the wheel" and "enlightened" for "living in darkness." The emperor is naked, and we are asked to compliment him, praise him, accept him, and undress ourselves right along with him.

It is chaos. And chaos typically threatens our mental and emotional stability. When our mental stability is threatened, we find ourselves feeling anything but freedom in our minds and in our souls. The sexual freedom we think we have is nothing more than disguised emotional bondage. What we all need now is true sexual freedom—a freedom that is only found in the wisdom of the cross.

Reclaiming that freedom is about understanding that sex is beautiful, sex is sacred, sexuality is something divine, and marriage is an ultimate expression of all that is perfect. The majority of the world seeks this ideal whether you admit it or not. I know I was.

There are no real negative consequences, or downward spirals, in choosing to seek purity mentally, spiritually, physically, and emotionally. It is the better way. It is the enlightened way. It is the way of anybody truly awakened to the truth about this dark sexual bondage we have been sold as sexual freedom.

In the emotional aftermath of all this chaos, casual encounters, infidelity, and the commodification of sex have all led to emotional distress, feelings of emptiness, damaged self-esteem, wrecked marriages, and messed up children and have created abandonment issues and brokenness in alarming abundance. We have all lost.

The emotional and psychological consequences have been overlooked for far too long, and scholars and feminists alike, when discussing these movements, are finally seeing that somewhere along the way perhaps the Christians had it right.

Sadly, I am not certain that Christians truly *believe* we have it right because I don't regularly see Christians successfully standing for purity over impurity. And when I do see them, they sound like parrots of a truth someone told them *about*, rather than harbingers of real *wisdom* as to why God values us so much, even when we don't value ourselves.

Many Christians have gone along with these misguided revolutions and supported the wrong movements, not realizing we are somewhat lost at sea on the issues today. We too have earned for ourselves mental health issues, anxiety, suicide, and depression by not recognizing the lies we are sold that glamorize impurity. We too have fully embraced culture and all of its manipulations, while complaining and accusing everyone else of doing so.

In short, many have sold out the Bible to be "woke." Have you?

Navigating this evolving and confusing sexual landscape has made us all pansies. We have shrunk back from a battle we need to be fighting. I don't mean fighting against people. Because *broken people are the aftermath*. We are the damage produced by the sexual revolution, and we are the *broken* born of the feminist movement.

People have problems, complexities, wounds, and damage from all our shared history regarding sex and sexuality. People need our prayers, our understanding, our love. Just as much, they need our truth *lived* out loud. They need us to be who *we* are supposed to be in the face of what they tell us is *their* truth. Because *they* believe their truth just as sincerely and deeply as *we* believe *ours*. But only one of us is right.

Who are *they*, you might ask? *They* are the world of people out there who don't understand that purity is the revolution that is rumbling, in a new way, more so today than ever, under the surface of our desire for emotional attachment, real connections, and committed love that lasts.

Why and how did all of this get sold to us in the first place? How did we fall for the lies hook, line, and sinker? How could something that is so ugly, with such ugly consequences, catch us all so off guard that we are now reeling in our bondage knowing we are not free but terrified we can never return to freedom? If we ever really had it at all.

Well, let's consider a different kind of landscape that has been glamorized step by step, agenda by agenda, ignorance upon ignorance, one movie and TV show at a time.

CHAPTER 3

MEDIA DRIVEN

Social Media, Music, Movies, Ads, Books, and More

There are a ton of TV shows we can look at and a mountain of media to prove my point—that the media is the biggest co-conspirator in making sex anything but sacred.

I think of my childhood excitement on Friday nights, which were reserved as family viewing nights. We couldn't wait to watch *The Brady Bunch* and *The Partridge Family*. These shows offered clean, wholesome family fun. It may sound cheesy, but there is something to be gained from the family values that predominated even the 1970s landscape. Crime was lower, family dysfunction was lower, there was prayer in schools and a sense of national pride, and young people certainly seemed happier.

Life wasn't perfect, and I had problems, of course. I was being sexually abused during this period of my life, but at least I had an escape to a better family and a better life through the TV shows I watched. They gave me hope. They didn't try to sexualize me further or abuse my mind with confusion to forget the fact that sex was for married people and that it was beautiful and created children.

Even the off-color jokes or sexual innuendos were hidden back then out of respect for the sacredness of sex. I am not being a prude. I am a fairly hip person who has, for better and worse, nearly seen it all.

By my twenties, I was overly confused about sex. I was trying to figure it all out without any real guidance or people to talk to. I knew the over-the-top promiscuous sexuality the world was engaging in didn't seem right. But I didn't understand the Church's view of sex or sexuality at all either. It seemed archaic to just tell young people, *"No!"* We just answer with *"Why?!"*

There was no middle ground. There was no *me* today to say to the *me* of *yesterday*, "Hey, little girl, wait. You want to understand the beauty and power of sex first. You want to know what your identity is—before your sexuality is even important. You are going to find someone great, and he will love and cherish you. And when you have sex on your wedding night, it will be beautiful—and then you will create a family. But wait until you understand what sex is, why it's sacred, and why you deserve the sacredness it was created for!"

In hindsight, I wish I had someone in my life who was open about sex and its power and the right way to use it and the wrong way to use it. I wish there was someone who would've explained to me what sexuality really was and what that meant to me as a girl and a growing young woman.

Instead, I approached my twenties already damaged by my abuse and the books I stumbled upon in my mom's room as a child that were, unbeknownst to me, the chic books for chic women to read at the time. They were called erotica. In hindsight, this was likely a word for the pornography that began seeping into mainstream media culture back then.

Before I became a Christian, my mind was in an early war with my own sexuality and what sex was because of exposure at a young age to these inappropriate books.

I knew as a young girl when I would thumb through these books that the stories of love and romance they spun caused funny feelings in my body. They tapped into a sexuality of sorts, or at least sexual feelings. I would always sneak to read them. In hindsight, I guess I knew there was something wrong about my reading them. Perhaps, there was even something wrong about the most important and admired woman in my life having them. Were they ok to read—or not?

These books always made women the object of desire. The more desirable to men you were, the more important a heroine you were. On the covers of these books, the men were always handsome and the women beautiful. It was pure fantasy. Packaged and sold and bought by me hook, line, and sinker. I wanted to be desirable. I wanted to be the women in these books because they seemed like important women to be.

Today it's no different. While I marvel at any young girl who would want to be Kim Kardashian or Cardi B, they exist.

So at the risk of sounding like the old people sounded when I was young . . . *what happened?* How did we get to a show like Netflix's *Sex/Life*, which is essentially soft porn, not to mention hardcore pornography—which is being watched by millions?

Easy.

It started with books, and then grew into a multi-billion-dollar industry that could expand, unfettered by feminine expectations of honor and commitment or a man's need to be responsible after sex for his actions, his children, our equality, or respect.

How? The media. The gift that keeps on giving.

At this point, if we look at what pornographic media has done alone, we could devote an entire book to it. More on this later, but it is sadly true, and not at all surprising, that more men watch pornography than women. This takes what the sexual revolution started and puts it on steroids while at the same time destroying any of what the feminist movement said was going to give us equal rights and protections. We are marginalized at best on a constant basis in media today as we are presented as naked paramours of sexual lust.

All the while, the media buffers all criticism of itself while promoting the worst forms of sexual abuse ever—the kind that looks glamorous and cool. The kind we easily rally for because we want to look like the characters involved. We want to live like the characters involved. We want to feel excited and experience the things we see and hear on TV and in the movies, and the selling of sex and sexuality is so forced upon us that you can barely escape its agenda to normalize what God would call abnormal, no matter what you watch.

The fact that it *feels* as if we are being *told* that we *have* to recognize something, or someone, and see life a certain way, feels like the forcing of an *agenda*. And honestly, I don't think people do well with forced agendas of any kind. That's a big problem for freedom-loving people. And sadly, the media seems to exist only to glamorize and normalize agendas forcefully.

Historically, art has always been a voice for the marginalized. The art communities have typically been communities of broken and compassionate people. Their art, when it's good, has sought to reflect those in pain, those broken, and those marginalized. It's a beautiful thing—until it isn't. And it isn't when we create fantasies as truth, especially when children are involved.

Children are capable of finding their own truth as they grow up. But while they grow up, the truth they should be given must come from their families alone. Not from the media. Not from their schools. Not from strangers. It is a God-given right that we steward our children. And for a believer in any faith, you know this includes stewarding your children in the faith of your family.

Part of my stewardship over my son involved navigating what he watched on TV, listened to on the radio, and read in books. The Bible says, "bring them [children] up with the discipline and instruction that comes from the Lord" (Ephesians 6:4, NLT). And "Train up a child in the way he should go, And when he is old he will not depart from it" (Proverbs 22:6, NKJV).

You have a responsibility to train your child in how to live and think. You are called to care for your children's emotional well-being. Since I was greatly damaged by my early exposure to media, I took this responsibility very deeply. This is not a responsibility you can ask any parent, especially one who gets it, to share or give up to anyone.

As I grew up, I dove into music, movies, and TV shows to escape the pain of my sexual abuse. I became very creative because of the escapist way my mind worked. Yet this ability we have as young people to escape into alternate realities is precisely why media can be so dangerous when left unchecked and out of balance in a child's life.

When nobody is there to explain or to guide, a young person is left to experiment with what they are seeing on TV or hearing in school and is often left in a place of totally unsafe behavior.

Nobody explained to me that the behaviors of many of the people I saw on TV and in the movies were incorrect. If it wasn't clear who was the bad person and who was the good, I took the creator of the show's word for it. *But how is anybody, besides God, to determine who is bad and who is good?*

What worldview a creator of a TV show had was not something I questioned until I learned that people have agendas, and they don't always line up with my biblical worldview about how I think God views sex and sexuality.

I remember getting engrossed by the series *Scandal.* As I watched it one year with my two nieces, then ages fourteen and seventeen, I stopped the show in the middle of an episode and looked at them both in horror and said, "Uhhhh. We are aware that Olivia Pope is a horrible human for having an affair with a married man and that Fitz is an adulterer, right? And we get that they are both liars and cheaters and that this show is selling us an affair as if it's the love of the ages when it's completely wrong?"

The irony of their ministry-immersed auntie watching *Scandal* with them dawned on them as they saw me squirming in my gorgeous butter leather reclining chair in our movie theater. The humor in my realizing that I was possibly endorsing the sin of this TV show by watching it with them was not lost on my precious nieces, whom I love as if they were my own daughters. We eventually all laughed like crazy, once I made it clear that what we were watching was *sin. Glamorized, agendized, and sanitized sin.* I needed to state it clearly to be sure they didn't fall into the fantasy created by confusion—and the confusion created by fantasy—all because of a TV show.

We talked and eventually went back to watching, but we all knew where the line of truth was and that the show was totally unacceptable in nearly every way. It's not always this easy or clear—*and* we shouldn't always be watching. I admit this just to say that there is rarely an Auntie Cynthia to stop the moment and say, "Hey this is a fantasy, not a fairytale that ends well, and the consequences of this bad behavior are the same as the consequences of all sin—not good."

Life isn't just like it is in the movies, and rarely do people who live recklessly survive.

Sex and the City: The Point of Departure

There are certainly many more shows we can discuss, but none so powerfully shaped a generation or two, including mine, like *Sex and the City*.

I was living in New York, and it was an exciting time in my twenty-something life. I had gotten my first job on VH1, when it was lightning hot. We all became famous and successful because of its specific moment in time as the music channel that was still all about music when MTV was becoming a reality TV show-driven monster. Shows like *Storytellers* and *Behind the Music* documentaries and VH1's Music Cares initiative dominated the landscape in New York City. And, for a time, I dominated VH1, and therefore New York City's landscape.

I started my career and was quickly voted an "it girl" by *The National Enquirer*, the tabloid of the day, with my pick of designers to dress me, my pick of men to date me, amazing girlfriends, and VIP access to one red carpet event after the next—nightly. And plenty Manolo Blahniks!

Wait! What are *Manolo Blahniks*?

They're a ridiculously expensive and beautiful shoe that every "it girl" coveted. They are a bit of a cultural icon themselves, as they became famous right along with *Sex and the City*. It's kind of like who came first, the chicken or the egg? Well, with Manolo Blahniks it's like who came first, Carrie Bradshaw—or the shoe? The *shoe* was a must have. The *show* was a must watch. And together it was a lifestyle *MUST*!

I was well acquainted with Manolo Blahniks—the shoe that essentially became the show's fifth character. Then, I became friendly with Candace Bushnell, the woman behind the show.

By way of media history, Candace Bushnell created a humorous column for the *New York Observer* called "Sex and the City" in 1993. It was based on her personal dating experiences.

The TV series, created by then "it boy" executive producer Darren Star, together with Candace, would revolve around Carrie Bradshaw, played by Sarah Jessica Parker, Candace's alter ego of sorts.

I remember being at an event one evening for HBO. I hosted a show for them called *The BUZZ w/ Cynthia Garrett*, and on it I regularly interviewed the casts of HBO's hit series. Nobody else mattered in the world of HBO except HBO shows and its stars, so my job was rather a dream. In terms of TV, we were the "it girl" TV channel, and we dominated television with hit movies and shows.

On that night, I was seated next to "SJ," as my producers referred to her, and Chris Noth, also known as Mr. Big on the series. The show was just launching, and Chris leaned over, winked at her, and whispered, "It's all about you kid, you're about to become a huge star." And boy was that prophetic! In fact, everyone affiliated with the series became huge stars.

The main cast included not just Parker, whose lead character was a freelance writer and fashionista known for her unique sense of style and her weekly column on relationships and dating in the city, but also Kim Cattrall, who played Samantha Jones, an independent and overly sexually liberated public relations executive. Kristin Davis also portrayed Charlotte York, an art dealer with traditional values and a longing for *true* love. And Cynthia Nixon played Miranda Hobbes, a career-focused lawyer who often approached relationships with skepticism.

The series garnered significant attention for its candid exploration of relationships, female friendships, sex, and modern dating in a cosmopolitan setting. The phrase "modern dating," in hindsight, was just code for *sex, sex, and more sex.* It tackled various social and cultural issues while offering a humorous and often insightful look into the lives of its characters. The show was New York fashion forward, particularly Carrie Bradshaw's eclectic wardrobe, and it became iconic and influential to fashion brands everywhere.

Sex and the City received critical acclaim and achieved a large and dedicated fan base. It spawned two feature films, as well as a prequel television series. It was rebooted by HBO Max in 2021's *And Just Like That.*

And just like that . . . Carrie and company were back in 2023 bringing us their view of life, sex, and sexuality—today. And, *while it may be enjoyable, should we all be scared?* Yes! And not just scared of *this* new series, but scared of every movie or TV show that goes further and further down the increasingly more and more impure bunny hole in desensitizing us all to the beauty and sacredness of sex.

Sex and the City was the national anthem to the sexual revolution and the poster child for what the feminist movement wanted us to believe. Yet it was all a lie. The four women, if left to their own devices, would have ended up old, alone, and plausibly suicidal. In the reboot, they are all old, mostly alone, and how on earth they aren't suicidal that at fifty-plus they are as spiritually stunted, emotionally confused, and slimed with impurity as they were in their thirties, is beyond me. Their lives today look tragic to me twenty years later.

But in my young adulthood, nowhere did I want to live, love, and look more like the characters on TV than in my love affair with the hit HBO series. I, like millions of women, somehow really related to Carrie Bradshaw. She was a completely unhealthy girl living a completely unhealthy lifestyle. And it was made to look fabulous!

She was my point of departure from reality and the point where impurity rather won over my mind. Of course, my body and soul followed. All of us—your girlfriends, daughters, sisters, friends, and wives—wanted to *be* her. But *who* was she? Did we ever even care enough to ask?

We didn't *see* Carrie's unhealthiness. Her sad and lonely attempts to get love often bordered on desperation and resembled our own unhealthiness. We never asked *why* Samantha was so sexually promiscuous. We never asked how Carrie's friends were all so broken in their attitudes toward life and men. Why were they so confused and eventually jaded and struggling? We never asked why they were all so *messed up*!

What we wanted to know was as shallow as the TV show cared to let us know. We saw her clothes and her friends and her access and how cute the men were. *We never saw her soul.* Her soul, or where she came from, or what her parents did for a living, never mattered. She wasn't human. She was a fantasy. One that men desired. And the message was loud and clear that we exist to be *desired by men*. And somehow that's all that mattered. To be desired by men while wearing fabulous, expensive shoes!

Those shoes told the world no matter what walk of shame you did home each night from some guy's apartment, you were at least a success. Because your walk of shame was done in *Manolo Blahniks*!

Carrie and her *Sex and the City* companions were sold to us as the ideal girls next door who had sex like men and lived to talk about it. While they provided an ideal that we all bought into, they sold us a lie that I dare say we have all lived to regret.

Dressing up sin in a beautiful dress and very expensive shoes does not remove the damage it creates. Many of us learned this the hard way. Many women today look amazing on the outside while their hearts are broken and their souls are scarred on the inside.

Now the subject of articles, debate, and historic analysis for everything from its fashion to its portrayal of female sexuality, *Sex and the City*, for better and worse, has become a cultural icon. Yet millions of us question whether it simply helped destroy culture in terms of male-female relationships, damaged women for generations to come, and glorified impurity in ways so appealing we all wanted a taste. Please be aware. That's good media at its finest!

In short, it isn't the job of the media to educate us on what sex is—and isn't. Nor is it the job of the media to monitor how it should be seen, used, or viewed by viewers and listeners. It is your job to educate yourself. Where, you might ask, does this education come from?

Let me take a flying leap into my faith by saying all education about sex and sexuality is found in the owner's manual for your life. If you believe you have a Creator, then that Creator, like all creators, will have created you with an intended design and purpose.

Just as *Sex and the City* had creators who wrote their series with a narrative, you have a Creator that wrote the series of your life with a narrative. That narrative looks nothing like the one provided by the *Sex and the City* writers. Your Creator's narrative is found in the Bible. A book that existed long before the book, from Bushnell's anthology of columns, that spawned the hit TV show.

Ironically, the Bible has more viewers even today than *Sex and the City*. Although the media is working hard at eliminating the Bible's narrative of sex and sexuality from the fall line-up, it cannot eliminate the Creator or His narrative. He has written the real narrative for your life of purity—not impurity. Your role in His series doesn't look like *Sex and the City*, nor does it resemble many of your other favorite TV shows. While you may feel aware of this, please beware. Because it's easy to become that which you constantly watch.

Maybe there actually should be some responsibility on the part of those who create these shows to think about the effect they will have on society as a whole. But whatever you feel about that question of societal responsibility, our view of sexuality should not be left to the media to *impose on us*—just as we shouldn't impose our view of sex and sexuality on each other. We are not victims unless and until we choose to be, and as free people we fully need to take responsibility for ourselves and our choices.

But that's not the case today. Much is being imposed on all of us all the time, and it is time to say, ENOUGH!

How do you do this?

By first understanding what's going on—because of what has gone on historically. By even reading this book you are clearly open to doing that. You have looked at the history of sex being turned into something created *for man*—rather than something *given to man from God.*

Then you stand up and change your thinking and your behaviors—now! You choose purity for your life and realize it begins in the mind to impact the body and the soul.

Then what? What's the red pill you need to take to unplug the TV sets and the TV shows that replay over and over in your mind? · In seeking your own understanding of the sacredness of sex and sexuality versus what has historically become more and more impure, you position yourself to win against the many battles being waged to steal your purity. And while TV, music, and movies are but one weapon used against your purity, your *consent* is another weapon.

CHAPTER 4

CONSENT

Take Your Money Elsewhere

D o we really consent to what the media sells us? Do we consent to the agendas they set that we don't necessarily believe in or want for ourselves and our lives? *Do we knowingly, and unknowingly, consent to the impurity sold us in the culture of lies we all live in?*

Yes, all day long! All day. Every day. In myriad ways.

Even if you have outwardly stated your desire to live more in line with what we once called "old-fashioned values," and even if you know the value of purity and seek to live purely, there is only one way for the juggernaut of agendas selling sex and sexuality in ever new and increasing ways to victoriously exist, and that is with your *consent*.

Whether informed consent or uninformed consent, whether intentional or unintentional, nobody can force you to participate in a game you no longer choose to play. Nobody can tell you that to be "woke" you must silently and knowingly go along with being asleep.

By doing nothing, you allow everything.

By saying nothing through your intentional and focused actions, you are allowing the media to tell you exactly how to think, feel, and view sex, sexuality, God, and history from a revisionist point of view. If you don't actively unplug, you are actively part of "the Matrix."

Even the new ChatGPT is programmed for the agenda "the Matrix" wants us to be part of.

ChatGPT constantly reminds you that it is not programmed to have a point of view. That is exactly its point of view—that everything is good to someone, and it's all good. This is the big lie. Truthfully, it is definitely *not* all good. Since it's not alive, it's only as pure as its programmers. ChatGPT reflects its creators' biases and is programmed to suit the nuances they create. There's that word again—create.

Good and bad, man cannot create without his specific set of life circumstances and beliefs filtering in. As you read this book, no matter how unbiased I may wish to be, my beliefs are filtering in, and I am using my experiences to teach you. My prayer of course is that millions of you will see the truth in my beliefs and help form the new revolution we need in our society today.

Elon Musk, who co-founded OpenAI, ChatGPT's developer, has stepped away. To be specific, according to a report from *Time Magazine*: "Musk worried that these chatbots and AI systems, especially in the hands of Microsoft and Google, could become politically indoctrinated, perhaps even infected by what he called the woke-mind virus. He also feared that self-learning AI systems might turn hostile to the human species."[1]

That means ChatGPT will never *say* that the feminist movement is a failure, or that the sexual revolution is a crime against purity and against mankind. It has no moral point of view. *Yet by not having one, it actually does.*

It will not denounce anything as sin. It will not conclude that purity is the best way for humans to survive and the only way for them to thrive. It avoids conclusions, making room for one truth—that it's ALL good. That is the premise of Satanism, by the way.

It is NOT all good. Not according to your original Creator or His original owner's manual. And if you have experienced moments of real delusion and pain over your choice to view something in the media that is perverse, or your desire to un-see something you've seen, or un-hear some music you've heard, or undo your sadness because your relationships never resemble those of Carrie Bradshaw or any other of your favorite TV and movie icons, then you *know* for a fact it's *not* all *good*.

In fact, it's all *bad* when it's impurity we are talking about, and life is never truly as it is in the movies you love so much.

In short, to choose purity in the media-driven age we live in requires that you prepare yourself to be canceled, ridiculed, called a hater, a racist, a misogynist, and a fool—to name a few. You must be ready to be canceled *and* shunned—just like your original Creator was when He chose to speak a truth that would end in death, dying for the messes we made and would continue to make.

But do you care if you ultimately win? Do you care if the fruit of your decision brings you peace and joy? Do you care if you gain freedom and you produce a family that walks in that same sense of freedom? If you don't care, then you are ready to withhold your consent!

If righteousness and purity become more powerful than unrighteousness and impurity, the truth is—everyone wins. We may not be able to effectively legislate righteousness, but we certainly can prove its effectiveness in family after family, community after community, and life after life. And we can reflect that victory for others to learn from in the media we create.

The media we *create*? Yes. Many of you are called to the creative spaces. Dare I say you have a responsibility now that you have unplugged to help others unplug. You have a responsibility to share the red pill with as many people as you can—just as your Creator did in the brief time He was here on earth.

We have the ability, the resources, and the mandate to go into the world and make disciples of men. Making those disciples is simple when you realize the power of the media and look at how powerfully it makes disciples of all of us. I was a disciple of *Sex and the City*. I was a follower and a believer, and I shared my beliefs with others every day in how I lived my life. And it was all wrong. It was a big lie. I pledged my allegiance to nothing short of the lie of impurity and reaped the wages of that sin for a time. We must create safer spaces for those behind us to live in.

Or would you have me believe that it's unfair for us *not* to create a space for the unrighteous and the impure?

This is what the media tells us all day through its constant producing and selling of agenda-driven sex and no-holds-barred sexuality. They tell us with every lineup on ABC, NBC, CBS, Netflix, Amazon Prime, HBO, Showtime, and on and on that we *must* allow the agenda against how we are created to exist—even though we know it's damaging, and we see the consequences and the harm.

We tell them by our inaction, "OK, no problem. If you show us a naked emperor, we will say that he has clothes on—when he doesn't." Millions of you have given over control of the narrative to others to create for you.

Consent

Our *inaction* is our action. Our silence is our yes. Our acquiescence to the agenda provided is our approval. And our participation through viewing, buying, and not boycotting by taking our dollars elsewhere is our acceptance—acceptance that enables them to create more filth and feed *us* more lies. It's like choosing to be suffocated by allowing someone to stuff your own socks down your throat.

I think many of us have become lazy and are willfully ignorant to what is clearly going on around us, like when I was in my twenties and didn't want to look at the reality of pre-marital sex according to the Bible I had actually *read*. Becoming enlightened to the mess means you now have to take a position and choose a side.

Once God turns the light bulb on you must choose to walk in the light—or choose to walk in the dark. Our consent is very much the battle we wage today concerning media. Do not question your Judeo-Christian values because others choose a different path. Bless them. But when you see them at the finish line, you'll know you've won.

I have spoken to countless Christians since the luxury fashion brand Balenciaga ran pedophile ad campaigns in which children were photographed in dark, sexual, bondage attire.[2] And then there was the Budweiser Beer trans debacle where someone thought it was a great idea to put a trans woman on a can of very working-class beer,[3] and the Target nightmare in which an apparent Satanist designed infant trans clothing equipped with tuck-ability to hide your child's sex to sell in the store.[4] Some Christians were literally giving me an excuse for why they had to run to Target that very week to buy diapers or whatever else they went to buy.

I blankly stare at these people who are the first to complain or the first to cry when things in life seem bleak, because I am shocked. You KNOW what's up. Do you live at all according to your so-called faith? Do you read your BIBLE? You have been *blessed* with money and choices. Why not go to Walmart? At least until they go totally woke too. Why not find somewhere else to buy your cosmetics, your household supplies, your food, your clothing?

Are you afraid that nowhere else exists, or that if it does it cannot be as big, entertaining, and accessible as Amazon or Netflix? I get that fear. But it's not real. In fact, fear is a moniker for exactly that . . . **F**alse **E**vidence **A**ppearing **R**eal.

I met a guy who started something called PublicSq (Public Square). It's an alternative to Amazon. Shop till you drop from those you want to support because of their values. More recently I was told about something called 2ndVote.com, whose motto is, "Your first vote is at the ballot box. Your second vote is with your wallet."[5] Patriot Mobile, which is in line with my thinking, gives you the same cell coverage as you would have with big companies, yet your money will never go to things you disagree with as a Christian or conservative.

When it comes to media and entertainment, which includes the goods we watch and the goods we buy, our first vote may be at a ballot box, but our second vote, and our most powerful one, is with our *wallet*. We live in a world where the real god is the almighty dollar. Money. It's the root of all kinds of evil. Stop serving it.

There are options out there waiting for us to "just say *no*" to the current compromised options that seem so big we think we can't win. We *can* win—by voting and spending differently in every way. David beat Goliath, folks. When did we forget that we Davids *can* defeat the Goliaths we face daily with our faith and our God?

It is possible to seek out the platforms and agendas that align with your values. It is possible to find places to shop that support those of us who see the power of purity in our world. *We have to.* We control billions of dollars amongst us Purity Seekers. We are a revolution against this force-fed denial of what is best for us as human beings when we band our dollars together.

Telling us that sex is unsacred, and that sexuality is chosen by *individuals* and not created by God—or worse by a school board that shuns parental involvement on any level—is criminal abuse. Some teachers have used this forced media agenda of sexual freedom in your *children's* classrooms. You cannot just lie down and take it! You cannot allow your acceptance to be implied because of your participation. It's time to homeschool, fight for parental choice, and force schools to have to compete for your dollars.

No matter how old you are, you are not too young to participate in the changes needed. You are not too young to plan a life according to the values you want. You are not too young, or too old, to withhold your consent to the agenda by buying elsewhere.

Whatever you call yourself—conservative, moderate, centrist, Christian, Jew, Protestant, Methodist, Baptist, or Muslim Americans—if it's purity you seek, then you must take your money elsewhere. We must shut down what we don't want and replace it with what we do by the sheer power of our financial position.

We may never all unite over our idea of God, but we can certainly unite over our understanding of what is right and wrong, good and evil, sick and twisted, and pure and impure. We can come together in understanding that family, monogamy, and purity in our lives create a better world for all of us.

Target has been hurt by the boycotts. Budweiser has been hurt.[6] Let's hurt them even more by taking what they need to create their poison away from them—our money! It's not as Herculean a task as you may think.

I love movies and TV shows and great books and magazines. I am such a child of the tube that I often get overwhelmed wondering if I too can ever unplug from "the Matrix" myself?

After years of counseling broken, lonely, lost, desperate people, I know that unplugging is the lifesaving first step toward actual identity and freedom. Sadly, we often figure nobody else will unplug, boycott, or just say no, so why should we not enjoy life as it is? Many fear that the beast is too big to defeat, and nobody really wants to give it up anyway, so we will all just continue to complain and do nothing. Forever.

But if we each continue with this thinking, things will never change—for you as an individual, and certainly for us as a society. The truth is that this change begins with one person's decision at a time. If I do my part and you do yours, the ripple in the pond will spread across the oceans.

"The Matrix"—being the media conglomerate that own your favorite TV shows, make the movies you love, sell the music you want to listen to, and design the clothing you like to wear—grows bigger because we are afraid we are too small. Can we really take our money elsewhere and be happy if we unplug from "the Matrix" called media? Can we choose the red pill called truth and purity? THAT is the question. I believe the answer is yes.

One TV show at a time, one film at a time, one store at a time, one designer at a time, one artist, musician, and actor at a time—we just unplug. We don't participate. We take our money, our eyeballs, and our ears elsewhere. *Or nowhere at all.*

We could choose to *live life purely*, even for a month, rather than watch, listen, or accept someone else's twisted version of life on TV. Our choice equals the changes we desire. Whether you like Donald Trump or not, he was right. It's all fake news. Even more so, it's all fake media. Until it's not. And we can swing it back to "not." We can force the telling of truth by simply not participating in the lies.

It's time to slay Goliath. It's time to beat the demon back into submission. He is running around on public display across our TV screens and in our schools, and we are acting like shocked schoolgirls instead of the warriors we have been created to be. We have focused too much on the people and not on the actual battle we are in. Have we forgotten that *we wrestle not against flesh and blood but against powers and principalities* (Ephesians 6:12)? There is a very real spiritual warfare taking place and we must war, with the weapons of *our* warfare, because *they are mighty to the pulling down of strongholds* (2 Corinthians 10:4)!

The obviousness of Christians' needing to do this should not need explanation. The Jesus we claim to believe in would demand that we shake the dust off our sandals and keep walking if we are not received in His name. If the values that He stands for, and the values that our faith aligns with, are not part of the climate that these large media corporations seek to also protect, then giving them our money is an act of total rebellion against sacredness, purity, and God Himself.

I know now that the only victory over all of this that you will ever achieve is at the cross. At the cross, you find mercy, strength, forgiveness, and purity. At the cross, you find answers to every single question you'll ever have about the people and the world around you. At the cross, you will understand that your media diet is your choice to regulate and consume, and forcing your agenda on others does not matter as much as forcing it on *yourself.* You need to figure out what *you* believe and live what *you believe.*

What do *you* believe? What does your faith say about how you should *live?* Do you *believe* in purity?

When I realized what *Cynthia* believed, it included abstinence, honor, sacred sex, and a heart full of Jesus to navigate the world and everyone around me with *truth.*

This is the main reason anyone who knows me *knows* how bold I am about Jesus and my faith, and about what He has done for me that causes me to desire and want purity for my life—and for yours each day.

People can take many things from you, but they can never take your convictions or beliefs if you hold them strongly. Purity is a belief we need to hold strongly to combat the ferocious way those who promote impurity hold theirs. My reasons for calling you to a Purity Revolution have everything to do with knowing that God is real, and He has a plan for purity for us all that *works.*

To App or Not to App:
Consciously Coupling Today

I realized in the twenty-third hour that I cannot write this book without looking at dating apps. Are these dating platforms media? Are they social media? They are certainly social. But more than anything, like all social media in general, they are a function of people searching for connection in a technological sea of disconnection and non-reality. But it is so much more complicated than even this. *And should we consent to their usage?*

I remember when dating apps hit the scene. "In 1995, the world's first online dating website was launched in the form of Match.com. Lonely hearts rejoiced as they could now meet and flirt with potential matches without having to change out of their pajamas," as Kayla Kuefler wrote in Stylight.[7]

I was young when dating apps became a thing, so I totally dismissed the entire idea as one for desperate people who couldn't easily get a guy. I had always had an easy time finding people to date, hook up with, and waste time with, so I thought everyone had the same experience as me.

Historically, "looking back" to figure out how we are "here now" is required, as with everything else I am saying in this book. As Kuefler noted, "Lightning struck twice at Harvard when Facebook was founded in 2004 and MySpace began one year earlier in 2003. By the end of the decade, Twitter, Instagram, and LinkedIn were all part of the digital lexicon."[8]

According to the Pew Research Center, 70 percent of Americans are active on social media[9] and one-third of the country is online "almost constantly."[10]

As Kuefler noted, "When a little-known startup called Tinder was launched, an entirely new demographic of people took to online dating."[11] This thing I dismissed as a stupid, sad way for losers to meet people had become a social phenomenon, embraced even by a younger, hipper, crowd, and it was here to stay. Boy was I wrong.

Like everything else in life, it seems to be about the person doing the programming. In all of these apps, if you are approaching them purely looking to find your spouse, then I would have to say that having help editing out all of the people who are clearly *not* meant to be your spouse is rather intelligent. Maybe the app becomes your facilitator in establishing the godly guidelines you want to follow but aren't strong enough to do on your own.

A lot of time is wasted by all of us with people we know are not what God ultimately has in store for us. We waste time for a variety of reasons. Attraction is a big one. When you meet someone and there is an initial attraction, you may likely avoid all the red flags that don't line up with the core values you know you have. Yet, because you are attracted, you waste time getting to the inevitable end.

I've never used or even seen a dating app function, but I have to imagine that on a dating app, if you are using it correctly, you'd swipe past your attraction when a guy's good-looking face says one thing, but his words or descriptions say something totally different than what you want in your life.

For those who don't frequent bars and clubs and places where you may meet people, and even for those who do, isn't there something appealing about letting an algorithm edit out all the nonsense for you and narrow your pool down to people that may actually share your faith and your convictions?

I am saddened to say that many of the young men I see in churches would have been edited out of my experience. If you know upfront that your nice Christian boy or girl has zero issues with pre-marital sex, before the struggle with the flesh begins, that might keep you from professing Christianity while getting undressed out of wedlock.

What if you could edit based on finding only someone who shared your deepest conviction that sex is sacred, and you want to be honored all the way to your marriage bed?

Would you describe yourself on an app that way and trust God to bring the right connection?

These are the questions you must answer. What I am saying may be shocking to some Christians. But put your judgments aside and look at the intentions of the heart. Do I believe that God can bring you your spouse right where you are? I absolutely do. He brought me mine at thirty thousand feet up in the air. (More on that later.) Because by then, I was ready for editing and deleting everything and everyone that I no longer saw as assisting in the growth of purity in my life.

If you are committed to doing things right, and you are swiping left until you find the one person that you can swipe right to—whose values align with yours, whose commitment to purity aligns with yours, and whose desire to build a life on a foundation of monogamy and commitment aligns with yours—then perhaps even a dating app is an arena God can bless you in.

Why not?

By 2019, online dating became the second most popular way for couples to meet. Studies even claim that couples who meet online have "more satisfying relationships, shorter engagements, and lower divorce rates,"[12] according to the interesting report by Stylight. So "love them or hate them, but online dating platforms are here and by the looks of things, they're not going anywhere."[13]

I am talking about this subject here because it's a part of the aftermath of all the revolutions we've been influenced by historically. Perhaps dating apps are even the newest revolution. But if you use these apps *correctly*, you can navigate your way toward deeper and more meaningful connections and waste less time hurting and harming yourself while trying to navigate to more healthy relationships.

But none of it is about the app.

It's all about the condition of your soul. When your mind is polluted, your soul is polluted, and your behavior is polluted. Eventually, your attitude towards sex, sexuality, love, marriage, commitment, and monogamy will no doubt be polluted.

The fruit of your life is as healthy as the root system of your soul. Sometimes it is just a toxic soul, with toxic roots, expressing toxic fruit, that we see on social media and while using dating apps. Dating apps are not inherently bad. They can only reflect the souls of their users.

It is time that we take assessment of our own souls.

It is time that the lust of the eyes, the pride of life, and the lust of the flesh stop driving everything you do regarding the opposite sex. Unless the idea of purity is driving your use of a dating app, or any other type of media that can be used to meet people, then what do you expect?

Is it love fulfilled, or lust unfulfilled, that is motivating your swiping—left or right? The answer to this question will save you lots of wasted time.

CHAPTER 5

LOVE VERSUS LUST

Their Respective Impacts on Relationships

S ince media are so good at creating a desire in us for what we see, now seems a great time to talk about lust. You might also think about it as the great turning of lust into love, as if they are one and the same.

This is my compiled definition of LUST: *An intense desire for something, like sex. A craving that becomes irrational. Theologically, a sensual appetite regarded as sinful.*

While lust isn't a dirty word, it is a *strong* word. You don't have lust for something you don't *really desire*. Lust is a strong, powerful desire, and whether it's a noun or a verb in your life today, we lust for things we deeply crave.

For most of my life, I chased after love. For most of my life, I confused love with lust. Therefore, you can safely assume that

I was chasing my lusts and seeing it as a quest for love. I was the classic case of someone who used *sex for love*, often running into someone else who may have only been using *love for sex*.

In my twenties and thirties, with total societal permission to have sex, I experienced a growing pain in realizing that I wasn't getting what I ultimately wanted in each exchange. I really thought that it was necessary to feel lust in order to arrive at love. I thought that attraction could never be love if it didn't exist first. I was always so happy when I ached for someone's touch. That seemed exciting and real. A touch was tangible. Sex is tangible. The physicality of my relationships became not just commonplace but necessary in my thinking.

I didn't realize I would never find love until I stopped using sex to get it. I didn't understand that lust was simply that—lust. It wasn't love. In fact, when I found real love, I had already committed to abstinence. Finally.

I wasn't attracted in the first instance to the man who has become my great love.

So, I wasn't looking for love from him at all. I was drawn to his mind, his soul, and his spiritual knowledge about our shared faith. I had no lust for him, or anything else, when we met. I had only myself, and my vulnerabilities. Because attraction wasn't leading the way, I had my heart open and a desire to walk in purity and live with Christ as my guide. I felt very undesirable because of all this, by the way.

Yet I was so in need of something "*more*" than confused sex. I literally got out of a very famous and sexy actor's car one evening and said to him, "Stop. No. Thanks. But I am looking for something more." He must've thought I was *nuts*. *Most* would think I was nuts if you knew who he was. To be honest, I wondered sometimes if I was nuts as well, as I read magazine after magazine about him sleeping with a slew of uber-famous Hollywood actresses. Even as I read about him with all of them, I knew he wasn't the "*more*" I was in search of. *He* is never the more you are in search of.

In fact, when another good-looking young actor I was dating left my girlfriend Pam McMahon's home one evening years ago, she turned and looked at me and said, "Well, he's cute, how's *that* workin' for ya?"

I remember laughing with her when I said, "Oh man, it's not. It's not workin' at all. In fact, nothing about the way I am choosing relationships is working even remotely."

It was truly hilarious by this point. I had everything going for me and could only achieve two-year relationships. At two years I was bored and looking for a way out, so that was my ceiling. My famous line was, "If I'm so *fabulous*, why am I still single?!"

After years of working on myself, I now know why. My picker was broken. The guys I picked were broken. And more than anything, I realized one screaming fact that was taught to me by my close friend Ted Forstmann. Teddy shared that fact with me one evening over dinner. He looked at me and said, "Countess," a nickname he gave me when we first met, "at some point you realize that the one common denominator in all your relationships is *yourself*."

That simple, profound truth caused me to begin to go inside in a big way. Before Teddy died, I would finally peel apart my own brokenness and get to the core of why I was living so far beneath what God wanted for me. The one common denominator was *me*. I wasn't necessarily choosing wrong men every time. In fact, most of the guys I chose relationships with were good guys. But it was me. I picked them disabled, to cater to my own disability. What was that disability?

I didn't understand what love was at all.

I didn't understand that there was a real difference between lust and love. And I didn't understand that when everyone tells you to follow your heart, they're completely *wrong*. The Bible I was supposed to believe in says something completely different than "follow your heart." It says the heart is wicked and it's not to be followed at all because it's sick and deceitful (Jeremiah 17:9). It's wishy-washy and unstable. We are to use wisdom and intellect to reason through what is right. Whose wisdom? God's wisdom—not man's.

Purity, in the way I was thinking, and in the way I was living, was in last place to some very impure mindsets and habits. In not understanding what love really was, I didn't understand what sex really was, what its place in my life was—or why it is sacred.

Love and lust are two very different emotions that often get confused with each other. I know that for a fact. While both emotions involve physical attraction, the underlying motives and feelings are vastly different. Lust is a temporary feeling of intense desire or attraction towards someone. It is purely physical and lacks emotional depth. That's why it would always pass for me, given enough time. My time limit was two-years deep.

Lustful feelings can be triggered by someone's appearance, scent, or even a fleeting moment of physical contact. It is a primal feeling that is focused on fulfilling one's own needs and desires. It is selfish. It takes. It is not in it to *give*. It is in it to *get*.

Love, on the other hand, is a deep and complex emotion that involves a strong connection and emotional bond between two people. It is built on trust, respect, and understanding. Love is not just a physical attraction, but also an emotional and intellectual connection. Love involves caring about someone's well-being, sharing interests and values, and building a life together. Love is all about giving.

The major benefits of love versus lust are many and varied.

Love is about longevity. Love is a long-lasting and deep emotion that connects two people and can withstand the test of time, while lust, on the other hand, is temporary and fades over time. When the physical attraction dissipates, the lustful relationship will end because it's not built on anything deep or substantial.

Love is a selfless emotion that involves caring about someone else's well-being. It's about making sacrifices for the other person and putting their needs before your own. Lust, on the other hand, is a selfish emotion that is focused on fulfilling one's own needs and desires.

Love involves emotional and intellectual intimacy, in addition to physical intimacy. It's about sharing your thoughts, feelings, and experiences with another person. Lust, on the other hand, is purely physical and lacks emotional intimacy. Lust usually has built-in walls to shield you from being too intimate because of the impermanence of the experience.

Love involves trust between two people. It's about trusting that the other person will always have your best interests at heart. Lust, on the other hand, is often based on physical attraction alone and lacks trust. In fact, much of the time lust is flat-out scary, yet we go along in the shadows and put ourselves in danger.

Love is also all about commitment to another person. It's about building a life together and working through challenges as a team. Lust, on the other hand, is about commitment to yourself and what you desire in a moment. It has zero long-term intentions and isn't looking to build *anything*. It is often short-lived and always lacks commitment, which is totally unfulfilling in the long run.

Alternatively, love brings a sense of fulfillment and completeness to a person's life. It's about finding someone who complements you and brings out the best in you. Lust, on the other hand, provides temporary pleasure but does not bring the same sense of fulfillment or completeness. In fact, where love adds fulfillment, lust leaves you unfulfilled after the act is over. It's as if you are left *minus something* rather than with *something added*.

Love involves respect for another person. It's about valuing their opinions, feelings, and beliefs, while lust often lacks respect and is built on a selfish objectifying of the other person. They have something specific that satisfies what you want for now, but their opinions or feelings don't really matter.

Love involves open and honest communication. It's about sharing your thoughts, feelings, and concerns with another person. Lust usually lacks clear communication, because it lacks actual depth or knowledge of the other person and can lead to misunderstandings and misinterpretations.

Love is about growing. It provides an opportunity for personal growth and self-discovery. It's' about learning from another person and growing safely over time. Lust often lacks personal growth and can stunt emotional and intellectual development. Lust is about self-focus, not self-reflection. Without self-reflection there is no personal growth. Any self-reflection I ever experienced in situations based on lust were the ones I had going home in the morning when I questioned why I felt bad and asked myself if I deserved more.

While both love and lust involve physical attraction, the underlying motives and feelings are vastly different.

When I consider the many ways I have grown because of my husband, I know that I have never been fully loved by, or fully loved, anyone before him. He has inspired me, motivated me, nurtured me, and supported me through things that were often not great or satisfying to himself.

Lust will always be a temporary feeling of intense desire or attraction that lacks emotional depth, commitment, and personal growth. While lust can provide temporary pleasure, that temporary pleasure will often steal something of your soul. Your youthful glow will soon become a faded glory when your years have been built upon a foundation that shifts and changes and is never present. Love, and only love, brings a sense of fulfillment, happiness, and completeness to your life.

No matter what you have been told, no matter how the purity movements may not have kept it real enough for you to relate, you cannot build a society of lust. Love is different. Love is life. God is love. Nothing of God mixes with lust. He reserves only the real thing for Himself, His presence, and His blessings. Lust is never the real thing, no matter where it ends. Not that His mercy and forgiveness, in our messes, isn't something He freely gives, but you have to ask yourself why we spend so much time in situations where He isn't?

Society has made it OK, even glamorous, for lust to exist free of strings attached. So sex can exist free of any strings attached. But sex is something that *should* have strings attached. We *should* expect something in return for our bodies. Again, if our own hearts can deceive us, because we may be in a place maturity-wise, or knowledge-wise, in which we just don't know what our heart wants or needs, then how many times have you followed your heart into someone's bed and found yourself with a million woes?

We have been told in a dozen ways that sex can be had without commitment or repercussion. Of course, because for lust to exist peacefully there has to be a lie we believe and an erasure of consequences, so we don't suffer for what we want to believe in. We have birth control—and abortion, when desired—to erase our consequences when we mess up in our lustful pursuits of pleasure for a night—or a season. But we *should* value pregnancy and life much more than we do as a society. We *should* see that love preserves *life*—while lust makes room for *death*.

We see daily that sex sells. It sells because it inspires lust. Sex is worth something. It sells on Instagram, OnlyFans, in TV shows, books, magazines, and media. It is a commodity disconnected from its actual reality. But what we need to realize is that sex should not be disconnected from the reality that it was created for true monogamous partnership, which brings the safety we need to grow and flourish.

Sex joins us together with someone and makes us one. If that other person doesn't want to be one, we feel disappointed and taken from, and rightfully so. Sex is created for unity, just as love creates unity. When you have sex out of wedlock because your lusts have led you prematurely where you know you shouldn't be, it creates a disunity within yourself.

Job 31:11–12 (NLT) sums up lust quite nicely: "For lust is a shameful sin, a crime that should be punished. It is a fire that burns all the way to Hell. It would wipe out everything I own."

Yes, lust will wipe out everything you own, and certainly everything you value.

Reflect upon the situations in your life that lust has driven. For me, they've not been good. They've been selfish and stupid.

They've always involved unsacred sex coupled with a misunderstanding of my own value and needs.

Lust has as its focus in pleasing oneself, and it often leads to unwholesome actions to fulfill one's desires, with no regard to the consequences to yourself or to others. Lust is about possession and greed—having what you intensely desire now and having as much of it as you can—until you don't want to have it anymore. Lust is for children who can't control themselves, to be honest. It is a very immature deviation from love.

King David took his eyes off God, and in a moment of boredom they landed on a married woman named Bathsheba, naked on her balcony across the way. Did he instantly fall in love—or *lust*? You don't need to know the story to answer that one, I am sure. Lust drove him like a devastating fire that destroys everything it touches. He had sex with Bathsheba out of wedlock. Since she was still married, they both also committed adultery. The fire raged on, and he killed her husband so he could have her all to himself. He committed *murder*.

That was some strong lust at work. In King David's greed and his need to possess Bathsheba, he *murdered* a man, her husband Uriah. He had *everything* as king and every woman he wanted, we can assume. *But it wasn't enough.* It never is when lust is involved.

King David paid the price, as did Bathsheba. They lost their first child. David's *lust* destroyed everything he loved and valued when the child died. He accepted it as punishment for his sin of lust, which clearly encompassed the sins of pride, murder, adultery, rebellion, and so on. This proves unequivocally that an intense desire for anything outside of God will lead you toward Hell.

In an interesting moment of grief, when David was praying for his child's life, he, like most of us, likely realized he didn't deserve his prayers to be answered. He didn't deserve grace. What he deserved was *punishment* for the crime of his shameful sin. When God did not give him what he prayed for, he resigned himself to his deserved judgment—and repented. He then focused even more on living a life free of lust for anything outside of God.

In your choice to pursue purity, ask yourself if you're interested in a life of love—or a life of lust. One leads to death. One assures life. I am a Christian, and that informs everything I do in my life. But it didn't always. I was thoroughly plugged into "the Matrix" at one point in my life. And the damage it did is the very damage I preach against today. If you want a healthy marriage and a healthier life, then understanding how to avoid the damage is critical.

Hypothetical Love versus Hypothetical Lust: The Christian versus Non-Christian Girl

Let's look at a hypothetical scenario in different ways.

Imagine a woman named Sarah who is in her early thirties. She is not a Christian. She has been in a casual sexual relationship with a guy named Adam for a few months. He is not a Christian. They have great physical chemistry and enjoy each other's company in the bedroom. However, Sarah starts to feel disillusioned because she realizes that she wants more than just physical pleasure and unsacred sex. She wants to feel loved and valued by Adam, but he shows no interest in building an emotional connection with her.

Sarah starts to feel frustrated and unfulfilled, even after their most intimate moments. She realizes that lustful sex is not enough for her and that she desires a deeper emotional connection. She begins to question if she is truly happy with the casual arrangement she has with Adam.

Eventually, Sarah decides to end things with Adam and starts to focus on finding a partner who can fulfill both her physical and emotional needs. She realizes that she truly wants to experience love, and that sex alone cannot bring her the happiness and fulfillment she craves.

This scenario highlights the importance of understanding the difference between love and lust and how true happiness and fulfillment cannot be achieved through physical pleasure alone. In Sarah's thinking, as a person of no faith, she concludes that sometimes it takes experiencing what we don't want to truly appreciate what we do want. But sadly, she has no easy answer to the emotional damage she has experienced as a result.

Without a North Star, a compass, or a belief system bigger than Sarah's own wisdom as her guide, she may make this mistake dozens more times before realizing her flesh is weak and she cannot conquer it without having something deeper that she believes in.

Sarah as a Christian Girl

Now, let's imagine that Sarah is a Christian girl.

Sarah, being a Christian, understands that sex is a sacred act meant to be shared between two people who are committed to each other in marriage. She may have entered into a casual sexual relationship with Adam, thinking that it was OK because they had an emotional connection—even love. However, as time passes, she realizes that the emotional connection she thought they had was not enough to fulfill her desire for love and marriage.

Sarah likely feels conflicted and guilty about her actions, knowing that they go against her beliefs and values. She has shame and anger for compromising herself with a guy casually, just like Sarah the non-Christian. She knows that God created her for more, and she actually wants more from her relationship. She now feels cheap and used. She doesn't feel honored, and she isn't even honoring herself. She wonders why she doesn't honor herself.

She also feels disappointed in herself for not being strong enough to resist her own lust. She realizes that she is living in her flesh instead of in the Spirit, and this too causes her anxiety as it goes against what she believes as a person of faith.

Both Sarahs can use this experience as a learning opportunity. But Sarah the Christian sees a reminder of the importance of staying true to her faith and values. She can reflect on the situation and understand that true love and fulfillment can only come from a relationship grounded in faith and commitment.

She can turn to the Bible and be reminded that God made sex for the marriage bed and that purity in how she lives, thinks, and behaves is pleasing to God and protects her from feelings of shame. She can turn to her faith for guidance and strength to help her overcome any guilt or feelings of disappointment she may be experiencing.

She can also pray for forgiveness and wisdom to make better decisions in the future. Sarah knows that she serves a merciful God and that in her repentance she is made clean because He gives us joy for our mourning and beauty for ashes. She is not like Sarah the unbeliever, who really has no peace for her soul. Christian Sarah has somewhere to go for an understanding of what sex is really for and why it's sacred. She knows that seeking purity in her thinking about her life will help her to get it right the next time.

She has hope, after repentance, and a clear vision of what victory looks like the next time her flesh tries to get the best of her.

Christian Girl and Christian Guy

Now let's look at another variation on our hypothetical scenario. What if both Sarah and the guy she is hooking up with are Christians? They may both feel conflicted and guilty about their actions, knowing that casual sex goes against their shared beliefs and values. Even if they feel they are in love, they will likely feel worse because they know sex was created for marriage, and they are not married.

They will likely question whether they want to be married to each other at all, and if the answer is no, one or both will experience deep guilt for acting from physical desire and lust, not commitment or honor.

They may have some idea that they are damaging themselves by going against God's Word because they may understand that the Word of God protects and guides for their blessing, not for God's. He is God. He doesn't fall off the throne because they sin.

They will no doubt feel disappointed in themselves for not being strong enough to resist the temptation of lust.

They may have conversations about their beliefs with each other, or other Christian friends, about their values and the importance of staying true to them. They may also discuss their feelings of guilt and shame and how they can work together to overcome them.

In some cases, they may decide to end the casual relationship because shame and anger at the other partner exist for not being strong enough to have steered the ship correctly. They may blame each other for not helping each other to be strong in their beliefs about saving sex for marriage.

Often for Christian couples, the relationship will end because of the seed of sin they planted. It grows in an ugly way and damages one or both partners' ability to see the other purely, or to look at the other person as a spouse or parent to their mutual children.

Sadly, it can color the relationship with shame and anger for having helped each other engage in something they both see as a sin against their faith.

Alternatively, they may both repent and decide to continue the relationship but establish boundaries to ensure that they are not engaging in behavior that goes against their beliefs again. They may, through mutual repentance, grow and strengthen each other to walk through the journey to marriage in a stronger and more faith-filled way. God is merciful and offers forgiveness. A broken and contrite heart He will never despise (Psalm 51:17).

Regardless of their decision, they can turn to their faith for guidance and strength to help them overcome any guilt or feelings of disappointment they may be experiencing—with themselves individually or with each other. They can pray for forgiveness and wisdom to make better decisions in the future.

If they are committed to each other and to marriage, then overall, their shared faith can serve as a guiding force in their relationship, helping them to navigate the challenges and temptations of unsacred sex (sex outside of marriage) while staying true to their beliefs and values.

Knowing they want a marriage testimony, they will find each other to be a great help when one of them is feeling weak. They'll keep each other strong and focused on their desire to have it God's way and seek purity together for the blessings it brings. They will form a mutual respect for what their decision to walk in purity will bring to them as a couple and to their future children.

Overall, our hypothetical Sarah's various experiences—as an unbeliever, a Christian, and a Christian dating a Christian—can serve as a reminder of the importance of staying true to one's beliefs and values, especially when it comes to matters of the heart and physical intimacy.

There are consequences to be paid because sin has a price. Something dies when we sin. A relationship. A dream. Hope. The Bible warns us, "For the wages of sin is death, but the gift of God is eternal life in Christ Jesus our Lord" (Romans 6:23 NIV). Sexual sin can carry some deep and lasting consequences all the way into your marriage bed. Trust me. I know.

CHAPTER 6

THE MARRIAGE CHAPTER

My Journey to Thirty Thousand Feet

M arriage has been the easiest thing in the world for me *and* the hardest thing in the world for me. It has not been hard because marriage, monogamy, commitment, and partnership are hard. They need constant navigating and compromise, for sure. But I have always been a loyal person, so this comes easily when I determine that someone deserves my loyalty.

It's honestly not hard for any of the reasons I thought it would be. It's not hard because living with one person for the rest of my life is hard. It's not hard because hearing the same person's voice or sleeping in the same person's bed for the rest of my life is hard.

It's hard because of the damage I did to myself outside of marriage because I didn't value sex in the way that I should. I didn't seek purity for my life physically, mentally, or spiritually. And until I did, I didn't get it. The reality of my reality has made it hard.

When I was young and in my BC (before Christ) years, as I like to call them, sex meant little to me. I hid behind several walls that I used to protect myself. Sex was one of them. I thought I could have sex without losing myself, giving myself, or expecting anything in return. I couldn't be hurt if I didn't *expect* the oneness that was supposed to come with the sex. It was *hurt* that I feared, not sex. I wanted to avoid pain. That was easy without expectations.

This plan, of course, doesn't really work. Each time I may not have expected a commitment—but I certainly *hoped* for one. Most of us do. I hoped to be loved in the way I suspected love should be returned. The Bible says, "hope deferred makes the heart sick" (Proverbs 13:12 NKJV). Truer words have never been spoken.

Many unmarried men and women have "sick hearts" but act as if their hope deferred doesn't bother them at all. But inside it does. Inside, I believe we all understand the pain of hope deferred. And waiting for a love that is correct may not be something you even understand until you experience it. That's how it was for me.

Just as my non-Christian girlfriend's six-week rule made so much sense to me back then, so does the truth of the biblical view I am going to give you, if you'll give it a chance.

If you're not married, hallelujah—you have time to learn and get it right. If you are married, you have time to pray for healing and to press into the most incredible partnership situation that exists on Heaven and Earth.

Having one person to love, in the way I love my spouse, and one person who I realize loves me, beyond any other human that has ever known me, even quite possibly my parents, has brought me a confidence that I laugh at sometimes.

I laugh because as I explained to my friend Daniel one evening, when asked if I ever get insecure because my husband travels so much, I chuckled and said, "No, actually! No, because I know what he has because he has *me*. And no because I know what I have because I have *him*. And to be honest," I continued, "even with more weight on than I had in my twenties, and even with getting older, and the natural changes that age brings to your body, I have never been more confident of my beauty and my worth than I am at this point in my life."

This is the confident and certain joy the safe space called marriage brings. I have been and am free to blossom. So are you.

Let me preface the telling of this true story by saying that I was always one to question all things. I was never one to believe something because someone else said it. I have always had that strength of mind. I am so grateful for it. If you have it, you should be grateful for it too. It is the mind of a leader. Sheep follow. Leaders lead. We desperately need leaders today.

Understanding whether you are a leader or a follower is foundational to your ability to choose purity for your life in a world of those who've chosen impurity. It will help you as it helped me to make a bold choice to wake up, take control of your body and your self-esteem, and say no to the impurity that is sold to us as a way of life.

As I learned about purity, I was ready, willing, and able to make a hard pivot from the historic manipulations that I once believed were normal, and understand that they had been deceptions at best, and lies at worst.

One day I got on a plane after attending a party the night before. Now I must tell you that this party was kind of an eye-opener for me. It was a birthday party for two very, very dear friends of mine. Their parties are a thing of legend in Hollywood. They are big and over the top, and every year they feature a different iconic singer whose songs everyone would know.

This one was that much more unique because it was in a church that had been transformed into a lavish party venue, equipped with dark lighting, loud music, a red-carpet arrival, lots of celebrity VIP guests, and pedestals that were set throughout the church with drag queen go-go dancers on them.

Yes, I felt the same as you may now, but hold on for the story. It ends well.

The Party in a Church: "Jesus, Don't Come Back Now"

The main performance that night was by the most famous drag queen in the world.

To be honest with you, when I arrived and I started walking the red carpet to get to the door of the party, I was immediately struck by the fact that I was going to a party like this—in a *church*. I remember thinking to myself as I walked inside, *"Please, God, don't let Jesus come back and find me here!"* I felt bad and super conflicted about a party going on inside a place that was built originally for worshiping God.

I quickly found the one person there I knew. I'll call him "Rick." He was someone I had worked for years prior as a younger girl on a big television network. Surprised to see him there,

I immediately wondered one thing—was he gay? Why is he here? Last time I saw him he was straight and married!

So I made a beeline toward Rick and latched on for dear life. To be fair, he latched on to me too. We both chuckled when I said, *"What are you doing here?"* I knew why I was there; I was there to celebrate the birthday boys who were longtime friends, one of whom had gotten me a job working for Rick years prior. But I was surprised when he looked at me and he sighed, "My wife and I got a divorce."

Oh. The moment of realization hit me. He was single and trying to enter the world of dating. I laughed hysterically at the fact that his first entry was at a gay party. He laughed also. An older gentleman, and a wonderful conversationalist, with whom I shared some fun memories about my first big network show, was a welcome relief for the night. We talked for hours, and at the end of the evening, we said our goodbyes, quite happy to have reconnected. We agreed we would get together for dinner.

Going home that night, I thought a lot about the fact that I had attended a party in a *church*! Something about it felt so wrong to me. I know that my friends there didn't know Jesus—*but I did.* So it wasn't about judging *them.* I was judging *myself,* and perhaps rightfully so.

When we know better, are we supposed to go along with those who don't? Or are we supposed to *not* go along? To sit it out? To abstain from participating? Only you can know with the Holy Spirit what level of participation you should have or not have. I believe this is why we must walk in constant communion with the Spirit.

Nonetheless, I do think often of our call to live set apart, to remain spiritually pure. 1 Peter 2:9 (NLT) is so beautiful as it states, "But you are not like that, for you are a chosen people. You are royal priests, a holy nation, God's very own possession. As a result, you can show others the goodness of God, for he called you out of the darkness into his wonderful light."

I knew one thing for certain back then. I wanted to show people the goodness of God. I always tried to be a light and love everyone. It was hard as I looked around me at so much that seemed so *against* God. It's amazing what people do when they just don't know the God who created them and loves them so much that He sent His son to die for them.

Up in the Air: Blue Skies and Sunny

The next day I had to get on a plane to fly to Philadelphia to do a product presentation to QVC, where I was then selling a line of jewelry. It was an inspirational fashion jewelry line called Love Conquers All. Come on guys—I know it's cheesy, but I was always this chick!

Speaking of always being this chick, no one in my world ever cared that I was a Christian because I was loving. I accepted everyone and everything they chose to do. I was open and didn't judge. Sadly, like a rabbi by the pool at the St. Regis Hotel in Bal Harbour once told me, perhaps I had become so open and accepting that my brains had fallen out of my head!

I boarded my flight with big black sunglasses and a big black hat on. I wore black sweats for comfort as I was headed to the East Coast! A long flight. The outfit kept most people at a distance because I didn't look very welcome to conversation or anything else, for that matter. I don't like it when people speak to me on planes. It's my place of solace. I don't want to have conversations there. The cell phone can't ring, and no one can reach me. Heaven.

I suppose, in hindsight, the way I was dressed also reflected my mood at that point in life. It was dark. I was searching for something, and I didn't know what. There was a piece missing, a hole in my universe. I was fine being single. I already had an amazing fourteen-year-old son, from a prior trainwreck of a marriage that didn't even last as long as my pregnancy and ended in a prison cell in Italy on my honeymoon. (That story produced my first book *Prodigal Daughter: A Journey Home to Identity.* It's the story of how I met Jesus in the first place.)

But back then something was missing. And it was missing on a soul level. Even with a son I adored and the blessings I had received, I wanted *more.*

So, I got on the plane at LAX. I took out a Bible. And I decided I was going to have a "come to Jesus" meeting on the plane. I needed to have a talk with God. As I was sitting there in an aisle seat in first class, I was annoyed. Why? Because I prefer the window. Something about the aisle makes me feel exposed. I like being cocooned in by the window.

A man in the aisle seat across from me leaned over after a few minutes. Having eyed the Bible on my lap as I was reading, he said, "So do you read that thing?"

I was immediately offended. From my perspective, things couldn't get worse. I was now across from some jerk who was going to make snide comments about the fact that I read the Bible?! I was not in the mood. I was not attracted. I did not want to interact with anyone on *that* day, at *that* time, in *that* moment! He stared at me, waiting for a reply. A few moments passed before I answered dryly, "Yes, I do." With that, I went back to my Bible.

After a couple of minutes, he nicely said, "Well, what are you reading?" I noticed he was wearing a wedding ring!

My next thought was, *Are you seriously hitting on me in the name of Jesus?! This man is going straight to Hell."* I gave him a sideways glance that said leave me alone. And, as if he read my mind, he stared at me for a few moments, and then reached down into a briefcase and pulled out a Bible and said, "I'm not hitting on you. I'm married. It's just that I read it too!"

He then said, "I have a word for you." I stared at him, confused. "Why don't you try reading Matthew 7:11." I read it, and it was as if a huge megaphone went off in my ear as I realized this was a divine appointment! The verse said, "If you, then, though you are evil, know how to give good gifts to your children, how much more will your Father in heaven give good gifts to those who ask him" (ESV)!

The scripture he gave me spoke exactly to the reasons why I got on the plane sad and hurting, wanting to have a "come to Jesus" meeting about where I was in my life. I just looked at him, unable to speak, and he smiled and said, "Don't worry. I'm married. I'm not hitting on you. It's just that I know the Bible and, if you read it," he continued, "why do you look so miserable? You should know that Jesus loves you." I began to cry.

"Jesus loves you" were words I didn't realize my thirsty soul desperately needed to hear. *He loves me.* This stranger on the plane was right. If I claimed to know Jesus, why was I so unhappy? And confused? I had a beautiful home in the hills above Mulholland and Beverly Glen. I had famous and wealthy friends. I traveled on private planes and walked on red carpets. I had everything—but something was missing. I knew it. I felt it. That *something* was deeply centered around three simple words. Jesus. Loves. You.

He loves you too!

Simply put, my life had become impure. I was surrounded by impurity. Mind, body, soul. I saw and experienced nothing but unsacredness. And it was taking a toll on my spirit and my emotions. I knew I was created for *more*, yet I was walking in *less*. It didn't make any sense. Until it would make total sense. And hearing that Jesus *still loved* me was an open invitation to get the *more* I was created for. It was an open invitation I grabbed as quickly as I could. It's the same open invitation being extended to *you* right now.

We talked about Jesus and His love and ended up getting into a Bible study about how to lead Jewish people to Christ. I began explaining to him that I had a best friend named Marshall. I had been praying for Marshall for the prior couple of years. I explained that he was such a beautiful friend and that I so badly wanted him to be saved and to know the love of Christ. I wanted him to know how special he really is, and that Jesus died for him. So, my first conversation with Roger, the stranger on the plane, was all about my Marshall.

Roger eventually asked his employee Andy, who was seated in the window seat next to him, to trade seats with me so we could get into a Bible study. He was going to teach me some things. So, I got my window seat after all! Laugh out loud.

As I sat on our flight from LAX to Philadelphia, he taught me using only the Old Testament. Using only the Pentateuch, the first five books of the Bible, with only the Jewish prophets and their words, he taught me all about the *prophecies* of Christ. He explained to me how those prophecies spoke of things that came true thousands of years later, through Jesus. As I watch the world around me unfold, and the years pass, many things are still coming true today.

It was amazing. I realized I was sitting next to quite the Bible scholar. And not just the Bible, but all religions. He was able to answer any question I had. This was incredible because I didn't know anybody who could answer my questions about my *faith* and *God* and *Jesus* and the *Bible*. I was yearning to understand how to live in the world and be the person that I wanted to be according to my faith.

I *craved* purity. The biggest part of my problem was that I had nobody in my life to teach me, or who was bold enough to intellectually confront me. I felt a general malaise, a lack of learning, a lack of growth in my life. I was missing the depth I knew was there, but I couldn't get to it. And here was this stranger, tapping into the deep places that I was calling out to, and explaining that I was calling out to God.

As we were approaching Philadelphia, he got a little anxious because we were only halfway through what he was teaching me for Marshall, so he invited me to dinner with him and his employee.

At this point, my single girl radar said, *"You know better than to talk to strangers and get off a plane with them in the middle of the night in Philadelphia."* I was a little bit fearful that I shouldn't just leave the airport with these two guys. He explained to me that he needed to pick up their rental car, and I explained that I had a driver. We were going essentially to the same area outside of Philly, where one of his longtime friends and biggest clients lived and had his offices.

I was going to QVC headquarters to do a product line presentation. So even though I was really anxiety-ridden and a little bit scared, I agreed to go with them to eat. All the while in the back of my brain I was plotting my escape.

"OK, there are two of them. There's one of me, but I'm getting in the car with my driver, so that means there are two of us, and two of them, and if anything happens, we should be able to get out of it." I also thought to myself, *"I will call my mom when I get in my car like I always do and check in, so she knows where I am, and what's going on."*

The two of them hopped in the backseat. For safety, I volunteered to get in the front seat with my driver. Roger instructed the driver to take us to some restaurant that he knew about downtown.

As we were driving, I called my mom to explain that I had landed and was in the car with two men, one of whom I had spent the flight talking to, and that we were going to get dinner. I told her that I would call her again as soon as I got to my hotel.

My mother immediately began screaming fearfully, *"Are you out of your mind? Are you not watching the news!? The Bikini strangler is at large! This man is out killing women all over the country and you are getting in a car with strangers?"* I was speechless. She was right, but she was also loud.

Roger reached his hand into the front seat for my phone and said, "Can I please talk to your mom?" So I reluctantly handed him my telephone. He asked for my mom's name, to which I hesitantly replied, "Linda."

"Hi Linda. My name is Roger. The Bikini Strangler! I am with my employee Andy, and I just wanted to say hello to the woman who raised such an incredible daughter."

Oh brother, how did he know? Flattery would get him *everywhere* with my mother. They began laughing and talking and all the tension seemed to ease out of my body, as we journeyed on to the restaurant.

We continued our unfolding of the prophecies that he taught me would help me proclaim Christ to my Jewish friends, especially Marshall. And when we were done eating, I dropped them at the rental car place to get their car. I went to my hotel and chuckled as I arrived there safely, alive, and without my bikini stuffed in my mouth.

I did give him my phone number because he asked me, when he learned that I was also a lawyer, if I would consider talking to his friend Brad Dacus, who founded an organization of attorneys that defends the rights of Christians to live freely in their faith. He explained that Brad was looking for people with connections to Hollywood to serve on his board. I was flattered to have a conversation with him because it was cool to think of my law degree having some use at that point in my life.

I was always one to love social justice and the fight for what's right against what's wrong. I was doing so little fighting for what was right *or* wrong in that season of my life that I welcomed the opportunity to be around more important people who were doing more important things than I was. I had one caveat: I told Roger I would happily have lunch with Brad but that he had to be at the lunch too. I didn't want to have lunch with a man I didn't know without someone there as a buffer. My mind was too capable of making up danger scenarios—a mind I clearly inherited from my mother!

Fast forward a few weeks. We all had lunch. Unbeknownst to me, Brad told Roger that day after lunch that I was to be Roger's wife. Now that wouldn't have made any sense to me at that point because I was still dealing with Roger as a married man, and being quite respectful of that fact. I had already been there and done that with married men and didn't want to go through the repentance over that again.

So, Roger and I became *friends*. I would often invite him and his wife and kids to various Hollywood events that I had tickets to. He would always respectfully decline or show up with one or two of his kids. Never his *wife*. She was always *invited*. He just never showed up with her. He always explained that she was busy.

We became friends solely based around the myriad of questions I had about the Bible. When he was able to return a call to answer a question, I usually had my list ready so that I could get them all out quickly. I didn't want to steal time from a married man and cause any weirdness. He was super respectful, and I am really good at being *friends* with guys, so it was a very easy friendship.

By the time we had lunch with Brad, a few weeks after my biblical flight, I was already dating Rick, my former executive producer from the party in the church. Things were fine. In the back of my mind, I had a million questions and anxieties around dating him, however. Would he accept my faith, would he accept my desire to be abstinent, was he too old for me, was I attracted to him, was his being Jewish an issue for me with my blossoming Christianity?

I enjoyed Rick's company, his conversation, and his laughter, but I was questioning the relationship deeply. Though ironically, his father's conservatism opened my eyes to much of what I felt intuitively about the world around me. The funny things and sayings and stories that he would share with me, that his dad would share with him via email, always made me think. His conservative political views surprisingly aligned with my Christian views and that comforted me on many levels.

For someone who wasn't a Christian, he lived a very moral life. We enjoyed a lot of wine and good company, but my growing friendship with Roger often presented me with tons to think about in terms of dating outside of my faith.

One day, I called Roger in a funk to ask him a question about my then young teenage son and how I was supposed to make him love Jesus, when I had only exposed him to an unreal world of secularism, wealth, and fame. As usual he said, "OK, well let's pray."

Anyone who knows Roger knows that's usually the beginning of every question or conversation. He is rarely looking to give you his answers; he's looking to get you to look at Jesus for your own answers. This is something I admire a lot about him. He points you to the answers you seek by pointing you toward the purity of the Cross.

So, we started praying. If you are a person of faith, you already know that prayer is just a conversation with God. It's a pouring out of your heart to God, but it's also listening to God and doing what He says. So, while listening, I felt God tell me to pray for Roger's *wife* and his *marriage*. So I did.

When we finished praying, it was unusually silent on the other end of the line. After a few moments, he asked me, "Why did you pray that way?" To which I replied, "I don't know, because God kinda told me to."

I was driving up Coldwater Canyon approaching Mulholland when he finally exhaled and said to me, "There's something I need to tell you, because after your prayer I feel like I'm being dishonest with you. I am not really married. Well, I am married, but I am separated, and my divorce is almost final."

I was shocked. We had been friends for months. I said to him cavalierly, "Why didn't you just tell me that?"

To which he replied seriously, "Well, honestly because I didn't think it was correct of me to discuss my soon-to-be ex-wife or our marriage with another woman!"

At this point, for any of you who know the intersection at Coldwater Canyon and Mulholland, let me just say this: I almost drove over the ridge and ended up somewhere down in Beverly Park. I was so shocked that any man in Los Angeles, California, had the integrity to *not* throw his ex under a bus to another woman that I literally almost wrecked the car.

I didn't know what to say, so I just said, "Wow, I am sorry, and I will keep praying for you guys."

From that point, I felt like our friendship was free to grow. We became the best of friends. That was firmly established, and I was happy with that. I even contemplated at times who I could fix him up with. I figured he should date, of course. After learning that he had been married since he was nineteen years old, an absurd fact to me, I felt like he needed what every other secular guy I knew needed—to get laid and get back in the game. To have sex.

At that point in my life, I assumed that's what all men wanted. After wasting years being married and monogamous, I assumed he would want to sow his oats. I lived for doing what I wanted, with whom I wanted. I couldn't imagine having given all that up to be married to one human being at nineteen years old and have four children. It all seemed so undesirable to me. Even as I wanted *more* spiritually, I didn't realize how much of what *was* needed was unraveling in my mind.

Meanwhile, I was still dating Rick, and had a wonderful friend in Roger to discuss my relationship with another man with. He once or twice kindly admonished me by reminding me that the Bible says I shouldn't be dating anyone I'm not equally yoked with (2 Corinthians 6:14).

I felt equally yoked with Rick because we came from the same work world. He understood my career, and he was pretty accepting of my abstinence, allowing things physically to be on my terms. However, I would come to learn that the equal yoking had more to do with how we were going to plow the field of life—not Hollywood careers or anything else.

Marriage is about seeing a mission field in front of you with someone else and having an equal desire about how to achieve the mowing of that field. It involves needing to walk at the same pace, grow at the same pace, have the same faith. Because that faith will impact your outlook on how you move and do things. That scripture would come to mean a lot to me in the very near future, when it came to my eventual *choice* between Rick and Roger.

Although I wasn't initially *attracted* to Roger in the usual "overwhelmed by lust" sense of the word, over time I began to see him *differently*. I respected his knowledge of the Bible and his commitment to living purely in accordance with God's Word. He had such a power and passion for his faith that it was awe-inspiring. This was all awkward and unfamiliar to me because lust, or something shallow, was usually an affirmation that I *should* get involved with a person. I was accustomed to physical attraction leading the way. A purely growing relationship was new to me.

I admonished him a few times to please *not* fall in love with me. I was afraid that he would. I told him that my guy friends couldn't help but love me on some level because after all . . . I was me! No shortage of vanity, clearly. He would laugh and assure me our friendship was safe. This gave me a real ability to be someone I wasn't usually comfortable being—myself.

I was only comfortable being myself with my closest guy friends. I reserved someone else for the men I *dated*. This is part of the impurity game that I see frequently between men and women. There is a retreat from authenticity. Nobody really gets the real you. You can't afford to give the real you because you can't expect to receive the protection and love the real you is actually desiring.

In order to protect ourselves, we hide. I see men do it. I see women do it. No matter how old or young. Dropping the walls and being the you God created you to be seems to be possible only when your commitment is to Him—and not outside yourself for fulfillment.

The first thing I would come to understand about seeking purity is that once you commit to it, you become quite comfortable in your own skin. There are no performance requirements to being yourself. A freedom happens in which you let go of the pursuit of anything except God. And in doing this you realize He will bring what you need when you are ready to receive it. I rarely see women—or men—cast their real, authentic selves as the star of their own lives, yet in the safety of living right, you find that you can. What's more important is that walking in purity is how you rise out of the muddy waters present in our culture of lies and walk into the clarity of saying "I do" with the right person, at the right time, and in the right way.

CHAPTER 7

CLARITY CAN COME IN AN INSTANT

Figuring Out "I Do"

Eventually, my faith-filled friendship with Roger would win out over my relationship with Rick. It happened simply and naturally. It came in a small realization that was a huge signal to me that I was picking men, in general, incorrectly.

I got in the car at about two o'clock in the morning one evening after dinner and a bottle of wine with Rick. As had become a habit, I picked up the phone to call Roger so he could wake up and talk to me until I got safely home. I have this thing, as does my entire family, where we fall asleep at the wheel while driving. So, when I am sleepy, I usually get someone on the phone with me to keep me awake. That someone over the months of dating

Rick—had become Roger. Roger woke up, and we began speaking as I started the engine of my car.

I was startled when I realized Rick was there knocking on the window of my car. I asked Roger to hold on, and I rolled down the window. Rick handed me my purse. "You left your bag." I took my handbag and said thank you, and I told Roger I would call him back as Rick was standing there. "Who were you talking to so late?" he asked.

I explained that I was speaking with my friend Roger, whom I had told him about. He seemed puzzled, so I explained further that when I would leave his house every night after two in the morning I was always sleepy, and I would fall asleep at the wheel. "I've told you that before." I emphasized. "I don't want to drive over a cliff on Mulholland."

"So," I continued, "Roger keeps me awake on the phone, so I make it home safely." Rick looked at me with some realization and said, "Well, I could have done that."

Suddenly, I thought to myself, *Yes, you could have—but you never offered.*

Things became clear in that instant. I was romantically dating guys who didn't treat me as well as my guy *friends* did. I caught the first wave of this revelation laughing at the absurd scene in a club, with Marshall, a couple years prior. As I looked around the room at all the shenanigans, the older women referred to as MILFs with younger guys, the desperation dressed up as cool, I thought to myself, "I am done. I don't want to be in a nightclub at forty doing this crap."

It hit me deeply and immediately that my guy friends weren't in it for any reason except—me. The *me* that wasn't in date mode.

The *real* me without lights, cameras, and a glam squad. A me I apparently didn't really know or appreciate at all. But they did.

I was conditioned to *perform*—like most women. I didn't think the raw, real, version of myself was good enough even though my guy friends clearly valued hanging out with the stripped down, vulnerable girl they loved.

I didn't act on anything at that point concerning my final epiphany at two in the morning with Roger and Rick. I just let it go. I was fine with the way things were, and I tried to stuff my expectations in a box as I was accustomed to doing. Rick and I were headed to the other side of the world—to New Zealand to film a television show that I was hosting for him.

Over the course of those weeks away, I would come to really miss my best friend, Roger—the stranger from the plane who would answer my Bible questions and wake up at two in the morning to talk to me as I drove home from my dates with another man.

Every day, from the other side of the world, while I worked and traveled, I found myself sending Roger text messages with my questions about the Bible, about life, and about my young son. He would guide me and counsel me and pray for me as always. After a few weeks away, we made an appointment to speak because I had a serious question that I needed answered outside of a text.

I needed to ask him a personal question about how much time he thought was appropriate to wait to have sex with someone. I figured he must've been dating and had some idea about how long he would wait before he would sleep with someone he liked. I was sure he must have some God-centered Christian version of the six-week rule my girlfriend had told me about years earlier. His would be the wiser rule, of course, because he was, without doubt, and still is, the wisest man I have ever known. With the deepest knowledge of Jesus and the Bible, and a number of other religions too, I needed to hear from Roger so that I would know how to view things with Rick. He was serious and was asking about a future. I knew marriage was on the table, and I wanted to be correct to him as well.

When the day for our call came, we fell right into conversation about the Lord as if three weeks hadn't elapsed at all. I eventually and hesitantly said to him, "Sooooo, hey, I have a question. Now that you are a single guy, how much time are you gonna wait to sleep with a girl you are dating?"

We had never had a conversation like *this* before. It was personal and awkward for both of us. But I needed a godly guy's opinion on this one badly. I needed to resolve this growing issue of what purity looked like and whether I was going to go "all-in-Bible" or not. I still wasn't totally sure what "all-in" looked like as it pertained to sex. I was waiting for some magic supernatural moment to occur in which I *knew* that I *knew* God's answer.

Roger was quiet a moment, and then he answered matter-of-factly, "Cynthia, I got married at nineteen, after being saved, and I was a virgin. I have been with one woman my entire life. My ex-wife. I don't plan to be sleeping with any woman until I am married to her on our wedding night. Because that's God's way, and I live my life surrendered to only one thing: God."

I sat there, silent. I felt stupid. It made such sense, but I was shocked at his answer. What about a six-week rule? This was *all in*. Somehow, I always knew it was, but I never believed anybody lived this way. I never believed anyone could.

Simply put, I had never met anyone with such a strong sense of who he was and what he believed in. His statement was powerful.

It was without doubt. It was committed, decided, surrendered. It was also sexy!

My response, after years and years of feeling slimed by the glamorously impure world I was in, was immediate and honest. I broke down in tears. Unexplainable to anyone but me and God—tears.

Then, out of nowhere I heard a swoosh, like the sound of curtains being pulled open. In a very cinematic moment of vision, I saw something like scales fall off my eyes as big red velvet drapes were pulled back.

In the same instant, I heard God's audible voice say clearly, "This is your husband."

It was that dramatic. It was that clear. In my seeking of purity, while stumbling, fumbling, and falling forward all over the place—God spoke. *How* do we deserve such grace?

I was now sobbing as it dawned on me who and what my future was. All I could think about through my tears was the reality that I had friend-zoned this man so hard—how could he ever want to step out of that zone? With *me*? How could God's will for "us" ever be achieved? The longer he was silent, the more I cried, unsure of any path forward in the conversation or otherwise.

I didn't know what to say. I needed to explain why I was crying, but I had no words. Mercifully, after listening to me for what seemed like an eternity, he finally, slowly, said, "Wow, I was wondering when you would get it. I have people praying for you all over the world." I could feel the smile, and the love, in his voice. He had known all along.

And just like that, I flew back to the United States, and we began the process of merging our lives into marriage.

It would be another four years of waiting for me doing inner healing work to be ready to walk down a sandy aisle on a beach. I realized that *Sex and the City* had really messed me up. It was not the Bible for a perfect, sexy, single life. It was the Bible for an imperfect and lonely life. It was the Bible for a bunch of lies millions of young women like me accepted as truth. And why not? Nobody else was pushing truth to me so effectively, convincingly, or glamorously.

Certainly, not the churches I was going to. Not even my mother, who was a bit starry-eyed about many of my romances with billionaires and Oscar-winning movie stars, God love her.

In talking to Roger about life and God and everything in between, he explained inner healing work. He explained Isaiah 61 and how Jesus, and only Jesus, came to set the captives free from their broken hearts in this broken world. I dove into that inner healing of my heart and my mind and never looked back. I ran after purity understanding that it was critical to my freedom on every level. It was not sex I had needed. It was just the opposite. It was purity. It was a revolution against everything this secular and impure world was selling me daily.

After much prayer, much counseling, much change, and transition, we were married on the beach in the British Virgin Islands on the island of Virgin Gorda, four years later. With just a very close family and friends, we rented four villas on a long stretch of beach and a boat and made a lot of wedding memories.

I very much believe that the purity I was desperately seeking resulted in God's audibly speaking to me. It resulted in my being able to receive the supernatural. I was ready. I was asking, no begging, God for it. I wanted two things above everything else: truth and purity. I knew that, as it says in John 4:23–24, the time had come for me to worship Him in Spirit and in Truth. This teaching implies that worship is not limited to a specific location or ritual but is rather a matter of the heart and obedience to His commands. My heart was ready to be obedient if it meant more of Him. I wanted *more*. It was more of *Him* that I was craving. Roger, like every husband, should be a conduit to that.

I needed to *know* that God was in my quest for purity in a world that taught me and nurtured me in impurity, because I was at a point where I wasn't looking for anything counterfeit. I wanted the real deal.

Within my marriage, as clearly as God affirmed numerous times that Roger was to be my husband and that there was, and has been, tremendous purpose in it, there have been challenges. Chief among them, I arrived to my marriage bed and was not a virgin.

CHAPTER 8

SAYING "I DO" WHEN YOU ALREADY DID

Breaking Ties That Bind

For those of you who have shared a similar journey to marriage, you will understand much of what I am about to say. My exploration of sex and sexuality with my husband was marred and discolored by my explorations of the same with other people. I know deeply that even if you wait, after having not waited, you will likely have stuff to work through. I want to be honest in sharing, so that when you feel your decision to seek purity will never net the results you want, you'll continue forward. There is no losing when you commit.

First, you'll likely deal with *shame*. I arrived at my marriage bed with a ton of it. The enemy loves to shame us for our sinful mistakes, no matter what our excuses are for making them in the first place. Sex was so surrounded by shame and guilt for me that it was hard to experience it freely and without all kinds of head trips. I couldn't easily make the transition from years of *unsacred* sex to *sacred* sex with my husband in a day. Why?

Because even in a safe space, with a safe man, I was damaged goods. I damaged myself by avoiding truth for so many years. I am blessed because the safety I have with my husband provided a very deep miracle, and that was that I knew I was loved *correctly*. So I knew I was safe to discuss what was going on inside me. In this way I was able to get his help and to pray through areas of brokenness and damage. He was instrumental in my getting healed and set free from years of mental bondage because of the impurity I had entertained in my life.

It is a proven fact that the number of sex partners you have impacts the quality of your marriage—negatively. The more, the worse. The fewer the better. None is the optimum number, according to the Institute for Family Studies.[1] "Nicholas Wolfinger, a sociologist at the University of Utah, has found that Americans who have only ever slept with their spouses are most likely to report being in a 'very happy marriage.'"[2]

Plain and simple, it is harder to be satisfied with *one* person when you have even a few comparisons. Sociologists want to say it differently. They look for ways to justify marriages being "OK" despite a multiple sex partner history. But the result is always the same; it's not the ideal. The ideal is you and your spouse and a world of beautiful discovery that you only ever experience together.

I think often of Song of Solomon (SOS 8:4) and the admonition in this book in the Bible not to awaken love before its proper time. There is a timing to the order of love. We have so much confusion surrounding what *love* is, that there is no wonder the premature awakening of love between two people causes such chaos and damage.

I mentioned in the beginning of this book that when man worshiped one true God, there was order. Chaos came with following many gods created by man to justify sexual sin. Song of Solomon is about order. From courtship to marriage to the assurance of love, it poetically presents a broad range of events and feelings in the days leading up to and during marriage, offering encouragement toward an enduring love amid the petty jealousies and fears sure to threaten even the strongest of relationships.

The lover and beloved in Song of Solomon represent Jesus and His relationship with His beloved—us. It's a beautiful book that is all about the incredible act of coming together, falling in love, becoming one, and living in committed devotion—at the right time.

There is a timing to all of this, and it doesn't begin with sex. It begins with respect and honor. This usually begins with friendship. The process is free of lust because the goal is not to achieve anything. The goal is simply to grow side by side understanding that if love occurs, there is a timing to when sex should also.

The exploration between the two virgins in the old film *The Blue Lagoon* is an incredible illustration of the latter. You may remember the film starred Brooke Shields.

Here you have two children who grew up on an island alone. There was no one else to explore, and nothing else to explore, except their friendship and the world around them. Eventually, when their sexuality naturally kicked in, they explored each other. They grew old together on that island, in a loving and intimate relationship, and all of us sigh with desire when we see the film because it represents a perfect ideal, perfect purity.

Yes, the real world off an island like the one in the film is much more complicated. But you do have a choice whether to participate in all the complications or not. Being friends and having love grow over time, until it is time to awaken that love and become one, is the ultimate way God would have us discover our one person.

The oneness I speak of, to be found in marriage, is created by the actual act of sex. And, to my point here, when you are to become one with someone else, the twisted reality that you have been one with two, three, four, or fifteen others is crazy and confusing. What do you do with this confusion? How do you break oneness with other people to be free to be one with someone else?

Because of God's tremendous grace and His joy when a child returns to seeking truth, your promiscuity or pre-marital sexual encounters of any kind is something a couple *can* overcome. You begin by breaking "soul ties" with each person you have ever been with mentally, spiritually, physically, or emotionally. You don't need to wait until you are married or engaged to do this. You should do it now. Right now. If purity is what you desire, then there is no time like the present to clean up your past unsacred encounters and be free on a spiritual level.

How can you do this?

A "soul tie" is commonly called a *"connection."* As we've discussed, the word is used on every "hook-up dating show" that exists today. We see men and women with beautiful bodies claiming to have a "connection." Those "connections" in those shows are almost always built on lust. The proof is in the pudding. Nearly none of these people end up in long-term fulfilling marriages. Yet for twenty years, since 2002 when *The Bachelor* first aired, we have watched them try!

The impurity of these shows is pure evil. It's why we often have visceral reactions to the few Christian contestants who have ever gone on. Most of them have behaved just like the world around them. While lost in the lie, they purport to live the truth. And the deception just continues. *What can you do to cleanse these "soul ties/ connections" from your life?*

Close your eyes. Ask God to show you every person with whom you have a "soul tie," also known as a connection. Wait. He will begin to show you people. Don't question it. Just receive. As the people come to mind, say out loud over each one of them, *"Lord, I repent of having impure unsacred sex with (NAME). Forgive me of my sin of fornication. Break the soul tie I have with (NAME) now, in Jesus's name."*

Do this for every single person that comes to mind. One by one. Do it even if you haven't had sex with a person who comes to mind, because "connections" and "soul ties" can form even if they are just mental or fantasy attachments to people, as well.

What you want to do is pray out loud that God would break each connection you have made with anyone that was improper. By breaking these ties, you create space spiritually for the right person to find their seat in your life.

Breaking these "soul ties" and "connections" also applies to whatever porn you are watching as well. You may not know their names, but you are engaging in mental impurity, forming mental attachments.

My sexual abuse as a seven-year-old girl marred the purity that would have helped me avoid so much damage and trauma in my life. But, at the end of the day, the things we blame as excuses don't matter as much as making the decision to seek purity with all our body, our mind, and our soul once we know we have a choice for our own victory to make too.

Life doesn't have to just happen to us. We can happen to life as well. A broken and contrite heart God will never despise or turn away (Psalm 51:17). If that's what you feel, your seeking of purity has begun.

A widely cited study by Jay Teachman suggests a correlation between a higher number of premarital sexual partners and a higher rate of divorce among women.[3] While correlation does not imply causation, and the study has been critiqued for not considering other contributing factors such as age, education, income, and relationship quality, let me say in my experiences counseling hundreds of women in small groups, and thousands through my TV programs over the years, that when a man or woman cannot shake the ties to their past sexual life, if divorces don't occur, bad marriages certainly do.

Those unbroken "soul ties" are simply connections to the lust of your past, the mistakes of your past, and the impurity of your past. *Why on earth would you want to carry any of that with you for another day?*

I have never seen anyone truly delivered of their past except those with a strong desire to serve the Lord and a commitment to seeking Him above all things. Freedom must become your purpose and passion in escaping being literally chained to the spirits you have become one with outside of marriage.

Past mistakes or decisions do not preclude you from seeking and finding fulfillment. Individuals can always choose to pursue purity in the present, regardless of their past. I mentioned Psalm 51:17 earlier. This verse is often interpreted in Christian theology as emphasizing the importance of sincerity and humility in repentance.

Most of us arrive to a true seeking of purity once we have been so damaged by our own sin, whether from our lack of knowledge, our confusion, or our rebellion, that our hearts are truly broken, and our repentance is truly authentic. What great hope to know that we live for a God who will never turn us away when we have come to the end of ourselves. In fact, at the end of yourself is often the place where God can finally begin.

Saving oneself for marriage and experiencing sexual intimacy with only one partner is deeply meaningful and fulfilling. Because it is meant to be. And while some people will say they need to have sex to know what they want in a marriage they are deceiving themselves. I have seen this delusion time after time. All it does is lead to more wreckage.

Continuing the same game that keeps breaking your heart is a nice illustration of insanity. It's a clear proof that you think perhaps you are in control of things and afraid to let go and trust God when the way things are done by everyone else seem to be inescapable for you. You feel that if you don't go along, you won't get along. This is simply your lack of faith and trust in God having a plan for your life. No matter what it is.

The discovery of your sexuality should be done in a safe space where exploration of what works, and what doesn't work, is covered by God to guide and provide for the union. That covering only exists within the one true safe space—marriage. Every other exploration is unsafe and out of bounds.

When you choose to go out of bounds, you are out there on your own. You may be successful at times and feel that you've not been harmed. You may even feel that you've had fun out there alone, where the wild things are. But what you won't feel is completely satisfied in the life you are living, because that life is not intended to completely satisfy you. Like drugs, it is just made for temporary highs and has no remedy for the lows, except to get high again. This is called addiction. From this place reason and wisdom are soon lacking.

The Foundation of Marriage: Three's a Crowd

What you *should* desire in a marriage has less to do with sex and much to do with *foundational beliefs* and *friendship*. If the sex were ever gone or interrupted for a period, it's the friendship that will last. It's the respect and the honor. There are couples that have been impacted by tragedy and cannot have sex. They stand strong as a couple with love and admiration because they were clearly friends first and lovers second.

Again, I marvel at those who have said to me that they couldn't imagine waiting until marriage to have sex, because what if they don't like sex with the person they're in love with? This amazes me. How little *faith* humans have *in God's* desire to bless them in *marriage!* Your knowledge of what God says should eliminate the need to *practice* sex if you have any knowledge of who God is overall. *As if practice makes perfect.* Christians should *know* that only Jesus makes us perfect, and He will for sure perfect our marriages.

Open communication, trust, respect, shared values, and mutual affection are key ingredients for a successful and satisfying relationship. If I didn't have that with my husband, we would never have navigated the many storms my past sexual encounters left me to weather. Having multiple sexual partners before marriage creates multiple impacts on your soul. Each time you engage in premarital sex, you become dinged or dented even when the "soul ties" are broken. Those dings and dents impact your marriage in far too many ways to state in one book.

Spiritual impact is a big one. Sex is created by God to be a sacred act that binds two people together in a profound and spiritual way. Having multiple sexual partners *clearly* dilutes the spiritual significance of this bond in marriage. This is why breaking "soul ties" with your past partners, crushes, sexual experiences, or even inappropriate mental ones is *urgent*. You need to put the importance of sex back in its place. You need to kick the counterfeit out so the real can sit on the throne.

Having multiple sexual partners can lead to comparisons in a marriage, which can create feelings of dissatisfaction or inadequacy in the marriage bed you are in—versus the multiple fake beds you have been in. We were created for one specific type of union, and whatever you try to use as a counterfeit for that specific union, ask yourself is it really, deeply, truly working for you?

Because marriage models God's relationship with you, it's about you and Him. Just as it's about you and your spouse. Bringing other people into your mind or heart is an abortion of the purpose of marriage. Two is company. Three is a crowd. Even when the three start in your thoughts, way in the back of your mind.

When those thoughts begin to grow, don't water them. Put them out with the word of God. That's what you do to maintain the purity of your life, mind, body, and soul.

How many jokes have you heard about having a lot of baggage? We all laugh about it. We think our luggage from past relationships and misguided thinking concerning sex and sexuality is normal. My girlfriends and I used to make cracks about our

"*Louis Vuitton steamer trunks of luggage.*" It was just a condition of life that we accepted. We were wrong. I was wrong when I felt that all the extra baggage was just part of who I am. It is, and it isn't. All your "stuff" should never become an accepted condition of your life. Your emotional baggage is not meant to be on the trip with you. You must start unpacking those trunks now.

A solid marriage requires minimizing emotional damage *before* you ever marry, if possible. Sexual relationships often come with emotional and physical attachments, as we know. We may have ended these sexual relationships, but the result is the emotional baggage that you have carried, or will carry, into your marriage. I have not seen a person who doesn't have some emotional consequences from premarital sex—especially when it was in a relationship that he or she placed *hope for more* in, or fantasized *as more* than it was.

I will tell you a bit about something nobody talks about. I have found it more common than you might think. I share it because you need to understand the extent of the damage that is occurring in the impure ways you may be living or have lived your lives regarding sex and sexuality. You also need to understand that if you are married, much of this may come as an attack against your marriage and your happiness. To have a strong foundation for marriage you need to eliminate the *spiritual uncleanness* that may have left some very real consequences lingering around your mind, body, and soul.

When you have a powerful experience of premarital sex, it can cause you to take on a spirit that will show up in your bed, often repeatedly as a past sexual partner, until you repent and are healed. I know this for a fact. In being open about it, I have encountered many women who have experienced this same thing.

For me, this spirit would take on the form of one of my past relationships, and so it was a familiar spirit to me. It was always with a boyfriend that I had a sexual relationship with. In my sleep, I was comforted. It would have sex with me in the dream. But I would experience it in a real way. The feelings, emotions, and the physical touch of a past person were so real it was as if I was with them. I brought this unsacredness into my marriage not understanding what was happening to me and too embarrassed to talk to *anyone* about it for fear of being judged or shunned—or worse.

I woke up one morning, early into my marriage, crying. I was desperate to have this thing that kept occurring stop. But I felt I must be crazy. I knew it wasn't right, but I didn't even know what I was experiencing, and I was definitely too ashamed to tell Roger. I found my courage eventually, and I looked at my husband and said, "I need to talk." I explained everything to him, not knowing how he would react, and he said, "It's a demon. Let's get rid of it." That simple. That safe. Remember, he is a man of tremendous spiritual knowledge and *maturity*. I can imagine others may have run for the hills.

Equally yoked with someone who could understand that I was asking for help, we prayed and got rid of this spirit that would take on the form of one of the men that I had a strong sexual "soul tie" with for years. The spirit was effectively raping me, continuously. Once married, it was cleverly bringing an open door to something impure and unsacred. But I refused the invitation. This was a door I wanted *closed*, not open.

Because I was sleeping, it was as if I had no will one way or another in what was occurring. Eventually, though, if my commitment was not to purity, and if I didn't understand the sacredness of sex and sexuality within my marriage, I may have just accepted this as something that was normal. Over time, I may have liked it, or even invited it when I was angry at my husband. Years in, when boredom wanted to creep in, it may have become an outlet of escape that I used, rather than live fully invested in my marriage to one man.

The path to impurity opens ever so slowly and deceitfully. You must slam the door in its face immediately. That means you must be willing to close doors in the faces of people and TV shows who want you to engage in impurity with them. All they're offering you is a gun with one bullet in the chamber. Eventually, you'll shoot yourself in the head.

You really must want this walk, and often you'll need to fight for it. But it's precious, and it's worth it. This specific form of attack against my quest for a pure life was the most confusing and real thing, that wasn't even real. Yet, it was very real. And the consequences of sin, even sin occurring in some subconscious place in my mind while sleeping, could have been the end of my marriage.

That's how deeply spiritual the power of sex and sexuality is. When distorted for so long it can become demonically empowered. Impurity breeds this kind of thing.

I was delivered of this type of spiritual presence sexually in my dreams the day I asked for help. The day we prayed against it, it *never* happened again. By this point in my life and marriage, I had learned to take spiritual authority over the enemy. My quest for purity has netted many results, and this ability to war and win against an enemy that wanted control of my sexuality for years is a huge miracle.

Fornication is the kind of sex that deforms us into less caring, less loving, less committed people. Sacred sex is the kind of sex that makes us better. It shows us in a special way what our relationship with God is like. Sacred sex has far more beautiful things for us than just fleshly pleasure. If you are willing to take on the risk of intimacy, which marriage is all about, you will know joys beyond telling. Joys that make the risk of love worth it, no matter the cost.

In my quest for purity, part of my victory was in confronting the spirits that had entered through the doors I had opened due to fornication and unsacred sex and evict them forever.

The gift of trust I have with my husband is monumental. If I didn't trust him, I could never have spoken to him about this demon showing up in our bed to have sex with me—while he lay next to me sleeping. I knew it was an attack on me and my marriage, and if he didn't trust me, he could never feel the confidence he has in our relationship being my choice forever.

That said, if one or both of you have had several sexual partners before marriage, it can lead to feelings of insecurity, jealousy, or difficulty in trusting your partner. I had so much emotional damage from premarital sex, that the strain an admission like mine could have had on my husband or on me could've been tremendous.

I know how most men would've reacted. Even spiritually mature men. But my husband, being a true scholar of the Word and having walked in purity for forty-five years, sprang into action to help a tortured daughter of God rid her life of myriad complex consequences, including the demonic, in her seeking of purity. Mind. Body. Soul. He understood purity of heart in how we are to compassionately love others, and he has loved me like no other. *When we discuss purity, it applies on every level, or success cannot be had on any level.*

Having multiple sexual partners can *also* increase the risk of sexually transmitted diseases. Duh. Some of these diseases go unknown and can have long-term impacts on health and fertility. This risk extends to your partner when you finally marry. While this risk can be mitigated with safe sex practices, it remains a concern. I have found, with countless young people, that no matter how safe they think they are, things like herpes get passed on inadvertently all the time.

There is nothing sadder than an unsuspecting partner who awakens to blisters and fever and learns that he or she has gotten herpes from the person they love. And that person may have innocently carried it from their last relationship. The cycle of loss in sex outside marriage is long and littered with victims who are now married and have regrets that last forever.

Conflicts with your values, or the family values you were raised with, can cause feelings that you carry for a long time as well. For those who strongly believe in saving sex for marriage, violating this belief may cause feelings of guilt, shame, or regret, which can negatively impact your self-esteem and mental health. These feelings will carry into your marriage and affect your relationship, as well. You'll feel as if the third person in your marriage is mental anguish, and that isn't a good thing at all. That anguish makes you feel as if you are a fraud and a failure. That too is Satan's deception. You are not a fraud or a failure. You are the daughter—or son—of the King.

If you have fallen, don't be ashamed. The only way to get up is with help and love and support. Most of us realize we are surrounded by that when we are trying to do the right things. I certainly did. I have such love for my husband who truly helped me walk out of impurity and into purity, one day at a time and one step at a time. If we cannot go "home" to our family, what does that say to every Prodigal out there?

Conflict with our own values and within our own community can cause shame, guilt, and regret that may feel insurmountable. And when people feel that healing their broken and shattered hearts and souls is an insurmountable task, they can become hopeless. Hopelessness can lead to suicide.

When the going gets tough in a marriage commitment, those who've had sex before will more easily throw in the towel, because their view of commitment has been impacted negatively. After you've had multiple sexual partners, you tend to view relationships as more casual and less permanent. Because they have been in your past. We get married for better and for worse. They are equal states of being. You can't enjoy one and flee the other. This is not a consequence of oneness. It's a consequence of being scattered in your oneness. A scattering that's easy when you've been one with many others. In short, commitment itself comes to mean that you are all in—until you are all out! All plans are firm—until they are not. How unstable can you build your life before you realize that marriage can only be built on a firm foundation?

If two people took the time to marry each other, the pitfalls of prior sexual encounters need to really be looked at truthfully as what they are—sinful relationships that involved unsacred sex with people God did not choose for you. In looking at the naked truth behind the impurity in these past relationships, you have a shot at seeing, understanding, and committing to purity in your future marriage. Don't romanticize your past relationships with exes as if they were fairytales and not, simply, relationships that ended.

When it comes to marriage the best statement is made in the opening narration in the trailer for the film *The Blue Lagoon* that I mentioned earlier:

Imagine two people who knew nothing about love—and so knew everything.[4]

That's what God wanted for us. Complete innocence and then discovery—with one person. Exploration without injury. Love at the right time. Sex in the right order. It is your lack of knowledge He finds beautiful when it comes to sex and sexuality. The innocence of purity, especially when you arrive to your marriage, is awe-inspiring. Your trust in God to help you learn what you need to learn, in the purest way, with the person He has brought into your life to stand in His place while you are here, is the miracle He wants for you.

Herein lies the beauty of marriage and why purity should be your ultimate pursuit. When your identity is aligned with how you are naturally created, your life blossoms.

CHAPTER 9

IDENTITY
The Place You Begin

T he fundamental issue with everything in this book concerning sex and sexuality, our historical twisting of it, and the ultimate deviance that prevails in the culture of lies we all live with is a result of identity. We don't know who we are. We don't know to whom we belong. We have no idea why we were created, why we are here on this earth, or what we are here to do!

"The Matrix" wants you identity-less so that you can blend into the identity it has created for you, leaving you trying anything and everything to have a sense of self.

Because of all the confusion around sex and sexuality, it is critical to talk about *identity*. In your search for purity and what purity means to your identity, there seems to be this lie that your sexuality and your identity are the same thing. They are not at all. You can engage in impure sexual behavior, or make impure choices, but you are never born with an impure identity.

How can we Christians expect unbelievers to know *their* identity when we so clearly don't know *ours* as we should? Worse, what we communicate about our identities is heartbreaking. It evidences a total lack of understanding. If we did understand, we would step up and take our rightful place in the world. So when looking at the impurity in the world around us, the greatest response to it is in knowing your identity in Christ.

NEWSFLASH: Sex is an *action*. It is a *behavior*. It is *not* your identity. Sexuality is a specific set of *behaviors* that you *choose* to live in. Even that is not your *identity*. Behavior is not who you are, just like your career is not who you are.

What you *do* is not who you *are*. Doing something bad does not make you a bad person. Doing something good does not make you a good person. I think about parents I have known who have struggled to get their kids to understand their identity as determined by their Creator.

What parent says, "My kid's just a drug addict, or a liar, or a thief, or even a murderer, because that's just who they *are*"? Any parent knows their child's behavior can change. And that's why all parents hold out hope for their children.

I too hold out hope for our society. I hope that we can see the need to look deeply at sex and sexuality and separate it from our identity. By doing this we can arrive at a mountain of truth that would impact our behaviors tremendously. By doing this we would understand who we are, whose we are, and why we were created.

People today insist that others should see their *identity* based on their *sexuality*. They consider *sex* a moniker of who they are. The confusion ensues because for those who understand what identity really is, it's lunacy for them to think that *your sexuality* or whom you *choose to have sex with* has *anything* to do with any of this discussion.

So where do you find your identity? Christians find it in the Bible. Others find it in behaviors, assumptions, and their own man-made wisdom. That looks scary and confusing today, especially since behaviors change. And man-made wisdom is, well, *man-made.* I choose to look to God who created me and wrote the owner's manual for my life to understand who I *am.* This does not disappoint.

It is also what I do with my own son, or the spiritual sons and daughters God has given me. I point them toward the manual for their life, written by their Creator—God. I use it to call forth their God-given identity and watch them flourish in who they have been since the day they were born.

Some are leaders. Some are warriors. Some are creative. Some enjoy science and have always thought about the world around them with scientific curiosity. How God made each of them is amazing. The beauty of them discovering it and learning to walk in it, *no matter what they do or how they may behave at times,* is that much more powerful.

As my son began to date girls, most of them beautiful models and actresses, I, like most moms, experienced my fair share of nervousness over the choice he would make for a wife—until I had a revelation one day about identity, Proverbs 31, and my role as his *mom.*

It struck me powerfully that a young woman's behavior, right or wrong, was not relevant to how I needed to direct my son. Every girl has her own journey to identity, and while I pray for all the young women he has ever been interested in—that they would learn quickly what God created them for, and why, so they don't get eaten alive in their confusion by a world of men who don't care about God, identity, or the sacredness of sex and sexuality—they are not my first concern.

While a girl may be all wrong, partially wrong, or completely right for my son, if he is interested, I point him to who God made *him* to be for his answers. If he gets his eyes on that, the rest of the equation answers itself.

Even if I think she's not sufficient to the calling on his life, because I see a certain mindset or value system at work in her behavior, I do not say it. I do not put a young girl down because in my *opinion* she is not smart enough for my son or not good enough for him. Again, it's not who she is that even *matters. It's about him.* I remind him of who *he* is.

I remind him of *his* identity.

I remind him that he is a future king and that he is at a place in his life where *he* is picking a *queen.* I explain that it is his duty to pick wisely, and to pick well, because a king knows what is needed for the task of ruling a kingdom. He wants a family and a woman who has the qualities, and the depth, to be a life-partner, a spiritual rockstar, and a mother to his children. That requires a queen with qualities that reflect the kingdom her king presides over.

Everyone focuses on the part of Proverbs 31 that is about the uber-woman who brings home the bacon and fries it up in the pan, all while raising the kids and being celebrated in the community for her hard work, her beauty, and her business acumen. She is amazing. And she is, of course, the type of woman I want for my son and for my grandchildren.

But God told me to dig deeper and focus on my own *role* in Proverbs 31. I take the wisdom set out in it quite seriously. My role, as his mother, comes before focusing on the uber-young wife's qualities, or lack thereof. My role as the future king's mother *is about pointing him toward his own identity first.* If you look at this chapter and study it, you will realize that the first half of the entire chapter is, in fact, the queen mother speaking to her young son, the prince, about how to choose a queen *because* he is the future king.

> The sayings of King Lemuel—an inspired utterance his
> mother taught him.
> [2]Listen, my son! Listen, son of my womb!
> Listen, my son, the answer to my prayers!
> [3]Do not spend your strength on women,
> your vigor on those who ruin kings.
> [4]It is not for kings, Lemuel—
> it is not for kings to drink wine,
> not for rulers to crave beer,
> [5]lest they drink and forget what has been decreed,
> and deprive all the oppressed of their rights.
> [6]Let beer be for those who are perishing,
> wine for those who are in anguish!
> [7]Let them drink and forget their poverty
> and remember their misery no more.
> [8]Speak up for those who cannot speak for themselves,
> for the rights of all who are destitute.
> [9]Speak up and judge fairly;
> defend the rights of the poor and needy.
> **—Proverbs 31 (NIV)**

Moms, we exist to call forth identity in our children. So do dads. My role has been clear from day one. Honestly, when I realized this about Proverbs 31, I was happy to discover that I instinctively realized, from the time my son was born, that identity requires *vision*. You must cast a *vision of identity* for a young person to grasp hold of it. Once you realize what identity is, it becomes easy to cast that vision. And once the vision is cast, it's easy to grasp and walk in. It becomes simple to make decisions that support your identity. It becomes simple to see what *behaviors*, or *people*, are inconsistent with your God-given identity and what actions are not useful.

If my son understands the vision for his life, he will pick a wife to suit that calling, even if he stumbles along the way. God created him to stand for certain things, and I have always tried to remind him of those things because they are integral to how God made him to lead.

The rest of Proverbs 31 continues with the queen mother explaining what a noble wife is and how difficult it is to find one. And it *should* be difficult to find one! Because once you clearly know the vision that is suited to your purpose on this planet, you are no longer looking *everywhere*. You are open only to that which fits in correctly with what you believe and where you are going. This spares tons of time and heartache with the wrong ones.

It's a beautiful and empowering thing to be confident enough to cast a narrower net more suited to your specific calling as a king—or a queen. By the way, scripture reminds us to go in through the narrow gate because the gate to Hell is wide and many travel it (Matthew 7:13). This may refer to Heaven, but how much more does it apply to marriage and purity? When you have a vision of your identity as determined by God, the road narrows to the one person who will ultimately walk the road with you, rather than the many who may simply be stumbling blocks along the way.

In the pursuit of purity in my life, I have found that nothing is purer than the roles we have that are God-given. When we pursue our God-given identity in Christ, we come to understand our identity in the world we live in. We know who we are in any room we enter and with anyone we date. We also remember who we are, to whom we belong, and to what we are called, even when our behavior is saying something different for a time.

Our instruction in the lives of our children is *everything*! It is meant to be so much more intentional, loving, and *wise* than it is in the world today. I have friends who essentially have let their sons and daughters just *grow up*. They have not *raised* them. They have not *guided* them. They have not sought the *wisdom* it takes to walk their children away from the wrong things and toward the right things.

Why?

Because, perhaps, mom and/or dad lacked an understanding of "identity" *themselves*, so their goals for their children were unclear. They didn't know what it meant to steward a child's identity, because they didn't know how to steward their own.

Many parents will have, sadly, perpetual princes and princesses who will not achieve their callings as kings and queens. They will not have been equipped to live life as successfully or as powerfully spiritually, so their choices for their own identities will be groomed and rooted in man-made wisdom.

Man-made wisdom consists of guessing, twisting the truth, and manipulating the facts to suit your desired circumstances. Man-made wisdom to me is justifying that for which man has no real wisdom. God engages in explaining *why you are who you are*, leaving you with no direction except the one He created you for.

Many parents have stumbled by placing importance on things spoken to their children by the world around them that they *thought* were examples of real identity. We were not created to place our feet in every direction, or to build our lives on the shaky foundation of feelings over facts. We have a rock named Jesus as our foundation. But if you don't know to *Whom* you belong, you have not yet found the definition of your identity in all things.

I love Proverbs 31 because here is a woman of godly wisdom who is guiding her son into his destiny by guiding him into an understanding of his identity. She casts a vision for her young adult. She calls forth that vision through her words, explaining what he will be, and in fact already is, to help him choose the piece of the puzzle that fits his God-given identity correctly. Therefore, that piece will fit his life correctly, and he can rule over his kingdom in the way he was raised to rule.

You can argue, fuss, and fight with your young people, or you can understand that they only perish for lack of *vision*. It's our job to cast that vision. That vision lies in showing them their identity in Christ.

I know deeply why so many conservative parents are angry and afraid of the trans movement that keeps taunting them with, "We are coming for your children." It's because intuitively we all know that it is *our job* as a parent to raise and instruct our children. In any kingdom, it's wrong to threaten any mother's cubs. You can come for many things, but get too close to a momma bear's cubs, or an elephant's baby, and you will die. We are made to protect our young. It is intuitive. When someone else is trying to usurp us in our most essential role, a fight will ensue. And the person who is not the parent will likely be the one to perish.

There is a fight over our children today that is against God's natural order. It is highly inappropriate for school boards, or men dressed in dresses wearing lipstick, to tell any parent they are coming for your child to teach them about their sexual behavior. A child isn't ready to comprehend adult sexual behavior, much less that which is outside the norm. Why would someone want to usurp any parents' authority over their own child? It's so out of God's order that it's demonic.

If you tell me that you are coming for my baby, it doesn't matter who you are, I will attack. Straight, gay, black, white, rich, or poor—my child is *mine* and always will be. My rights over my son are secondary only to God's. His rights over my son are sovereign, and He has chosen me to steward my son's life.

When you threaten the vision that a parent has for their child's life, especially when that vision is established in a true understanding of identity, you attempt to step into a place only God can stand in. No man in a dress, woman in pants, leader in authority, or teacher and union can ever stand in the place where only God can stand.

God is Lord over our children, and only He can tell us how to shepherd them and their identities. We won't all get it right. Some kids will suffer. But it is still no man's job to usurp what is divinely appointed about children and their parents.

When it comes to shepherding them in identity, purity is foundational. We must start doing our job and teaching them that purity is critical to identity. God is pure. Impurity is not God. He cannot exist as impure, nor does He reside with sin.

Your soul is your identity, your personality. And *your identity is created by God.*

We are the unique person that He made unlike anyone else. There is only one of you. There is only one of me. Not any of your "behaviors" can change your soul. How you have sex or what you consider important about your sexuality has *nothing* to do with your *soul*. It all has nothing to do with your identity.

I am absolutely devastated by the actual manipulation of women and men into abusing themselves with surgical alterations in the name of identity. With the desire to look better, or to be more attractive to the opposite sex, or to be someone else gender-wise, the reality is none of this ever produces *identity*.

If you study the life of Walt Heyer, whose organization Sex Change Regret counsels those considering gender reassignment surgery, you may change your shell to suit your desired look, or to suit your behavioral choices, but your core person still has the same issues post-surgery that existed pre-surgery. *You* are still the same you no matter what you enhance, cut off, or alter.

Yes, there may be a season of elation post-surgery. But as with all "highs," it will wear off. Then you are left asking, "What next? Why do I still feel awful inside?" Because no matter what you do—you are you. Your mind is polluted with a thought that drives you from the reality of your truth—into the deception of the culture of lies you are embracing.[1]

To add insult to the total abuse of all this, TV shows get created about it for the rest of us to be entertained. No wonder I sit and *cry* watching episodes of *Botched*, a show about the many grotesque appearances made by doctors who will perform surgery on people who need a psychologist and Jesus, not a new face, butt, lips, breasts, or gender reassignment.

The show is an example of how low the enemy will stoop to humiliate and destroy people. He deceives people into altering their God-given beauty and uniqueness, and then when he can get them into an obsession about it, he calls them to do more and more. It's never enough. Something else always needs to be nipped, tucked, fixed, deleted, or added to. It looks much like addiction as it sets in.

Eventually, these Frankenstein creations wander into the offices of two famous Beverly Hills plastic surgeons for help, because their procedures have been *Botched*. Thus, the name of the TV show. We watch as if watching a train wreck. And sadly, everyone laughs or is horrified by the Frankenstein creations of the many unscrupulous doctors around the world who enable sick people to do sick things to their bodies.

Don't we see that the illness that leads to all of this has begun in the *mind*? Not a person's body. Do we not understand that this has nothing to do with identity and everything to do with either some form of *mental illness*, or worse, an inability to see yourself as perfectly as God sees you?

Do we not get that the heart of man is broken and that out of the overflow of the heart we find men and women living impure and twisted lives while thinking impure and twisted thoughts? Our minds are ill. Therefore, our lives are ill. Then we make our bodies ill. And everyone laughs and pretends that the emperor is not naked. But he is. He is naked, and that's the naked truth.

Though we would like it to be different, it's not. It is just the same with trans people. Absent the one or two men who look decent as trans women, most of them have chosen to go from more attractive men to rather heinous looking women. There are some who are beautiful in appearance. I think Blaire White is very pretty. But, while you can sometimes hormone away the rough edges on a man to pass him off as a female, you cannot in fact turn that man into a *female*. And vice versa.

The manipulation of trans people is so sad that I cannot believe it. It is heartbreaking and fills me with rage against those who say they love them yet never point them at the truth. The medical statistics of the quality of their lives after castration, medicine, and all manner of surgical abuse are shocking. Yet nobody really cares. Not many will tell the truth or discuss it because when they do, they are called transphobic, hated, and persecuted with cancelation.

Those of us who love you because we know you are God's beautiful children and long for you to know Him so you can find your freedom are afraid to speak up too. We are afraid because in order to protect you, and to fight for you, we would need to speak the truth, and the truth will get us canceled, destroyed, fired, and harmed. The truth, even spoken in love, is dangerous. Truth has been weaponized in this culture of lies.

I deeply believe, from a place of love and a desire to understand, that silence is complicity. Silence allows these illnesses to occur and grow unchecked in a way that is not kind. We don't say it to the straight women mutilating themselves daily and injecting foreign objects into their bodies to appeal to men, satisfy their own delusions, and look like Jessica Rabbit or Kim Kardashian. And we don't say it to the trans people out there seeking to sell their surgically altered beliefs to children. As if any of these mutilations will lead to lasting happiness. As if impurity is seeking to destroy any attempt at bringing the purity of truth to this conversation, how can we say we love others and remain silent? But then again, how can we say we love others and talk so much mess about people who don't even know that according to the Bible they are in sin?

I speak knowing how difficult this conversation is to have and still be looked upon as someone who cares, but I am concerned that we are selling delusion to children, and that's just not right. Adults have the right to choose. Children simply do not. Children are to be shepherded by parents, and parents should never allow children to make life-altering decisions when they are *children*.

Kids cannot be trusted to vote, drink, or have sex until the legal ages of eighteen to twenty-one. Yet we live in a culture asking us to accept as normal these same children being allowed to change their *gender*? What is wrong with *everyone*? Children change their minds as many times as they change their socks, or their pre-pubescent crushes as they grow up. Yet, the fact that we would even discuss this as humane shows how insane and sexually in bondage the adults have become. Our nation has gotten sick from the culture of lies we live in to think this is even acceptable.

If you are a truth-seeker, then you will eventually stumble upon Walt Heyer, who I mentioned earlier—a man who lived as a woman for eight years before de-transitioning back to a man. In an interview with Walt, whom I have had on my shows before, he said the euphoria and presumed happiness that comes once you transition wears off in a few years, and all you are left with are your same mental issues, problems, and fears—but now, for most, you are mutilated and may have alienated many of your friends and possibly your family. This causes deeper depression than before the surgery occurred. This mental delusion, called "gender dysphoria" in Abigail Shrier's book *Irreversible Damage* (Regnery Publishing, 2020), is "first and foremost, a psychopathology—a mental disorder to treat, not primarily an identity to celebrate."[2]

It is the same with a generation of young women I see roaming around with butt implants. Many look so awful I cannot imagine they do not see themselves as I do. Yet they do not. They hide behind something external to create an *illusion* they want. And illusion has nothing to do with vision or identity.

At the end of the day, we all need to remember that perhaps you may get fake breasts, fake nails, hair extensions, wigs, breast implants, butt implants, or surgically altered private parts—whatever the case—*absent Jesus your void will never be filled.* Because only God is pure. And only purity fills the void. You must find peace with who you were created to be, and only then can you find freedom in your own body—just as it is.

Although it is often celebrated in the media, it is awful to see that someone you know is one thing is seeking with everything in them to be something else. I hurt for our trans brothers and sisters when I look through God's eyes. I do believe if they could choose differently, they would.

Sadly, many of you who understand the deep and lasting truth about identity, as determined by our mutual Creator, won't go near enough to what you perceive as "sin" to even explain to sinners about the God who loves, saves, and redeems. But how does anyone know the depth of Christ absent someone who will open a door and share it?

I don't judge or expect people who don't share my faith to get where I am coming from. I understand that they are living as authentically as they can, given what they believe or don't believe. Many are not aware we live in a culture of lies. Many think sexual behavior *is* identity. Many find sexual promiscuity to be sexual freedom. Many do not see the bondage they are in. This is why I try never to judge anyone—but to point them to God's truth. I remember when I too thought my sexual promiscuity was freedom and accepted bondage as identity. I too remember that it was *only* the Holy Spirit who succeeded in convicting me of my own sin.

Just as Pastor Chuck Smith opened the doors to the hippies in the 1970s in California, allowing in a revival for our nation where thousands of hippies got saved weekly, we too should be opening our doors to reach everyone. I didn't say open the door to a biblical reinterpretation. That's useless because only the *Gospel* can save. And there is only one Gospel. But there is a huge difference in sharing the Gospel and truly opening your heart while sharing the Gospel with those *lost* to the truth of it.

We are not walking in our identity as Christians. To walk in our identity would mean that our love would open the door for us to speak the truth we know, tempered with godly wisdom, to others who don't yet believe what we believe. Walking in our identity would mean we seek to first clean up our houses before looking at everyone else's homes with disdain. We lack power in our convictions about Jesus because we clearly don't believe our convictions have power.

We certainly don't seem to believe Jesus has power today. If we did, we would talk less, condemn less, and share the Gospel more. I have never lived side by side with so many people who call themselves Christians, or Christian leaders, yet are terrified to share the Gospel or pray for others in public. I have become disgusted by entire communities of Christians who gossip, slander, and judge unbelievers in ways so awful I question constantly why anyone would *want* to follow Jesus today. Why would anyone want to embrace the purity of Christ in their mind, their body, or their soul when purity can look so impure as it's presented by some Christians?

The answer is a giant hypocrisy. Christians believe they are right, but sometimes they never even share why.

Chuck Smith knew the power of the Gospel to save. And when everything he found disgusting and dirty and sinful landed on his doorstep, he had a choice to make. He had to ask himself what Jesus would do. Thankfully, He chose to do what Jesus did and sit down with the lost and the unsaved sinners and teach them about the Man who loved them above and beyond all other men first. He chose to point them toward the cross. And it was there, and only there, that they changed their clothes, their drug use, and their sexual behavior and found true freedom from the bondage they never knew they were in until they met Christ. It was there at the cross that they took off their sinful behavior and found their glorious identity.

CHAPTER 10

IF YOU AREN'T TALKING, WHO IS?

Family Time

I marvel at those who don't know the extent of what's going on in our kids' schools. It seems shocking when I have to show another person the number of viral videos that exist of parents in school board meetings protesting the pedophilia and pornographic literature being read to our children. *Are we so numbed by our media diet and distracted by our pursuits that we don't see that culture is educating our kids in place of us?*

It seems a lot of parents have become so complacent that they've stopped paying attention to what matters most. The children. Your children. Our future. You say you are afraid that "they" are coming for our children, and in many ways they are. But what does that matter if we are not working to promote, celebrate, and protect *our* values as vigorously as they work to promote, celebrate, and protect *theirs*?

If we are doing our job and teaching our kids what they should know about our faith, who cares what the enemy is doing? Whatever he is doing won't work against *us* because we know that "no weapon formed against us will prevail" (Isaiah 54:17 NIV). Be who *you* were created to be, a child of God born to live in purity, and your child will be the same! They hear your words, they watch your actions, and they judge the truth for themselves.

Every person reading this book knows a young person who needs a parental voice in their lives. They need an aunt, an uncle, a big brother or big sister, a mom, or a dad. I committed myself to conquering a huge problem—the lack of dialogue between young and old and the lack of "keepin' it real" by those of us who have been there and done that.

When sharing the truth and beauty of Christ's love isn't done in Christian homes with our own kids, then how can we ever see them walk in purity? They need to understand what purity is and what it really applies to. *You* can commit yourself to being a voice. *You* can focus in on a few young people who would love to feel the safety and confidence of understanding what the boundaries for a pure life are.

If identity is the greatest gift that you can give your child, then creating a home in which they can talk to you about anything—including sex, sexuality, and everything in between—is even greater!

I know that sex is difficult to discuss with your kids. I know it may feel awkward. I know that navigating sexuality openly with them today is beyond tricky. But again, one screaming question: *If you're not talking with your kid about sex and sexuality, then who is?* Dad, if you aren't discussing how a boy should treat your precious daughter, then trust me—her girlfriends are telling her, and nine times out of ten you won't like what they're saying.

My son, Christian, means the world to me. His name is Christian Abraham because I was praying for faith like Abraham's when I was pregnant and living through the personal circumstances that surrounded my son's birth. (You can read all about *that* in my first book *Prodigal Daughter: A Journey Home to Identity*.)

It has taken years of faith to raise him while navigating a world that has gotten more and more complex in its attitudes toward children, sex, sexuality, and morality. At the beginning of my journey with my son, I was given some amazing advice by a child psychologist in New York. She told me to answer just the questions he's asking when he asks them. Answering questions that he's not asking is mentally damaging.

Well, never have I seen culture trying to answer questions that kids are not asking like I see it today. You have to ask yourself why? *Why* is the world so interested in educating your kid about sex and sexuality? I can tell you why.

While they have confused your kid and implanted thoughts in their minds that didn't exist before their books, TV shows, and indoctrinating voices began to assert control, *you had stopped speaking*. You went silent. Perhaps you stopped really believing in what was once preached to you, so you don't even teach the good you know to teach. You have left your kids in a world of impurity without any understanding or expectation of what purity even is.

Newsflash: Some of you have kids that are associating their new identities with how they "present," what pronouns they choose, or what gender labels they desire—straight, gay, lesbian, or trans. They themselves desperately *need you* to explain and to set an example for them to follow. If you're too uninformed, too afraid, or too uninterested to talk to them about anything they may be going through, I ask again: *Who's* explaining all of *this* to *them*?

If you're not talking to your kids and explaining that this stuff that may affect their feelings is not about their true identity, then *who is*? If you are not talking about what it all means in the long run, then *who is*? I will tell you who is. The world around them. And the world around them is deeply rooted in *confusion*. There are even some in the world around them that hate them because they are Christian kids from Christian families.

Truth has very little place in the world today. And unless you fancy your kids hearing the opinions of a bunch of folks you may find untruthful, confused, or worse, you need to step up and do your job. We need to address our own. If you're not even asking *them* questions, then how do you even know what questions they need answered? There is much confusion we have all been born into, and it has magnified through time. We all need truth. But when we look at younger people, we need to recognize that we have a responsibility to help them *find* truth. They are our future, and our future has been corrupted by our past. Our history of sex and sexuality has provided an awful web to escape. We are the bridge from that broken sexual past to a brighter sexual future. If we won't be that bridge, then there are plenty of people in the culture of lies who will be. Except they'll be walking them in the opposite direction across the bridge. I was not ever going to let that happen to my son or any of my spiritual sons and daughters. No way.

Things were not as nuts in my son's school environment back when he was in high school as they are today, yet I do remember when a gathering at chapel at Campbell Hall in the Valley area of

Southern California was led by a *man* who took time to explain why he was now a *woman*. This caused my eleventh-grade son and his friends to giggle and laugh all the way home that day, as they repeated over and over—TMI, TMI. Too much information. They didn't care to know his story.

But I did.

I remember feeling a bit upset, as I thought to myself while we drove home, *"Why are they answering questions these kids are not asking?"* Then I remember being flat-out angry as I thought, *"Hold on, why are they answering questions that are mine to answer?"*

This moment ushered in a world of fear and reality about *how* sex is talked about to our children today. If we aren't the ones doing the talking to our kids about sex, sexuality, pronouns, LGBTQ issues, transgenderism, and everything in between, then we are leaving them to have these sacred conversations in an unsacred manner with potentially unsacred people. And usually with people whose beliefs and opinions are not grounded in wisdom equal to our own about *our own kids*. They're having sacred conversations with unsacred people!

How have we allowed our fear, inadequacy, discomfort, or lack of knowledge when it comes to sex and sexuality to silence us with our own children?

As if being sexually abused myself as a child didn't already leave me in enough fear of anyone taking advantage of my beautiful baby boy physically, I was now in fear of the world around him taking advantage of him and his friends *with its own agenda*.

My *agenda* was to raise a healthy young man who embraced our family faith and loved Jesus. That included loving others, even if they lived and loved differently. This was a perfect and good agenda. Upon reflection, it was not lacking. Why did his school suddenly feel it needed to round out my agenda or fill in its own details? I became angrier and angrier as I drove home from one part of the valley to my home in the Country Club Estates in Westlake Village, California. As a matter of fact, I gave new meaning to the phrase "angry black woman" by the time I pulled through the gates of my community with my son and a car full of his friends.

My agenda for him, or any of them, did not include conversations that would awaken lust or feelings prematurely about sex or sexuality *of any kind whatsoever*. The *world* was answering *questions* he and his friends never *asked*. It was providing information, undesired by him, unapproved by me, and unnecessary to his development as a human being at his age.

He was already a compassionate kid who loved everyone, straight, gay, or otherwise, so the need to force a conversation about how a man became a woman on him was sexual abuse in all its glory. And since I was sexually abused myself, I have major issues with the abuse of children. As I pulled into my garage that afternoon I was, in a word, *pissed!*

Sadly, sexual abuse is exactly what most children in classrooms are experiencing today. Forcing conversations on them that educate them about sexual choices, not their own, is confusing. Forcing them to act as if every option that exists in the world for them is an *identity to be considered* is a LIE. It's a polluting of their minds and their souls that awakens feelings and thoughts prematurely and is against every agenda that would seek to protect children. It is criminal.

In fact, my friends who had kids dealing with some of these issues were choosing to handle it privately with their own children. They were allowed dignity and given love and support at home. What manner of idiocy decided that this was a school issue?

As if the boys didn't already all know who was gay or lesbian at school. They rarely attached a word to it because they were just *friends* with people, *not gender labels*. They were already appropriate with each other and didn't need a school display provided by a grown adult whose conversation with a room full of minors should have been criminalized then—as it should be now.

When you are being told something that you don't want to hear, it is with one of three motives: to indoctrinate, to educate, and/or to stimulate. When it is forced upon you by the fact that you cannot get up and leave the classroom, it is now kidnapping—and an abuse of your innocence. It is classic sexual abuse. I find it odd that most of the inappropriate indoctrination in our classrooms is completely unsolicited and undesired by 100 percent of the children in class. *Yet why is nobody prosecuting?*

By now we should have all seen the video that went viral of the Reverend John Amanchukwu, who slammed school board officials in North Carolina for making a book which depicts various sexual acts available to children in school libraries.[1] The book is so illicit and pornographic it's shocking. As Fox News reported, "'If you don't want to hear it in a school board meeting, why should children be able to check it out of the school system?' he [Amanchukwu] said after officials cut him off when reading from the book. 'We have perverts that are perverting our kids, and you all sit back, smug in your chairs and celebrate diversity, equity and inclusion, but you (don't) want me to read it, so you can hear it.'"[2] Well . . . he read it. It's cringe worthy.

Or have you heard about "the former Missouri teacher who resigned after school administrators found out about her OnlyFans account"? "She told Fox News Digital that she's made close to $1 million by selling adult content on the website," according to a report from Fox News.[3] And this woman says she doesn't regret it at all.

And there is a case from an Oregon high school where an assignment titled "With Whom Would You Do It?" was given to students in early 2023. It "had students write the initials of *both* a boy and a girl in the class with whom they would be willing to perform various acts, including anal and oral sex," according to a report from the *New York Post*.[4]

Just for your information, as reported in the *Washington Free Beacon*, "Oregon is the latest blue state to embrace sexually explicit curricula. Thousands of Massachusetts parents in 2021 pulled children from sex education classes in which kindergartners learned about genitalia. Hundreds of Illinois school districts last year opted out of statewide sex education standards that directed teachers to instruct students about a number of controversial topics, including hormone blockers."[5]

In the earlier days of what is now an onslaught of TMI—too much information—I was determined to protect my son's innocence and purity for as long as humanly possible. I shielded him. I controlled the circumstances around him. I did my best to keep him *pure* by not acknowledging things that even *I, myself,* may have been doing that could've been seen by him as impure—*because they were.* I did not want him educated in such a way as to ever think wrong was right and right was unimportant. *Yet now his school was choosing to interrupt that very worthy goal?*

At first, I wouldn't *acknowledge* my own impure choices, or the impurity of thought that was rampant in the secular world, and I just hoped he didn't notice. I guess I figured if I was silent about things, he would assume they didn't exist. But they *did* exist. And they were popping up in his schools and in conversations with people I did not want to be the voice of reason in his mind.

I did everything except *talk* to him openly and honestly about sex, sexuality, and why purity was a powerful choice. If there is a naked truth behind sex, it is that a generation of young people are having it without any guidance at all from us as *parents*—and even less guidance at all from the Church.

My goals were worthy but ignorant.

I didn't understand the sacredness of sex then, as I suspect many parents don't now, so how was I to begin to help my young son navigate it? What I realized as a parent is that I hadn't sorted out the answers for myself, so I was raising him in an atmosphere of fear. I was afraid for him because sex and sexuality had hurt me, and I feared what it could do to my son. Fear is not a stable place to teach from.

I didn't know how to talk to him back then, so all he felt was my fear of the crazy world outside my Christian worldview. This clearly came through to him. *How do I know this?* A funny day in college years later showed me.

When my son was at the University of Kansas, our family had a big presence. A long, great story for another time. Suffice it to say, that while in my kitchen, full of his college friends one day, he made a comment about how I had made him think that if he kissed a girl, he would get her pregnant! Everyone laughed hysterically. I realized in this moment, that while his teasing of me for being overly concerned that he was going to be sexually molested, inappropriately touched, or have sex with a girl was hilarious—it was also awful.

Somehow, my gift to him was to cause him to associate sex with all manner of *fear*. Rather than equip myself to talk to him *about* sex so he understood what was correct, and not correct, I equipped him with fear and avoided talking at all. I left him to figure it out on his own by hoping he didn't figure it out at all. Like most Christian parents, I just wanted him to avoid sex and never question sexuality until he was safely married—then figure it out with his wife, who had better be a woman of God. Ha. How any of us made it until this point is a mystery!

I understand that my limitations surrounded my own experiences, as with many people, but we owe it to our kids to help them navigate the world around them. Open, knowledgeable dialogue is critical to facilitating their success in this world. They are hungry for answers when their questions arise. For many kids today their questions are arising early, simply because people with zero connection to them are interjecting their voices and opinions. Outsiders are instigating their confusion, and initiating their questions, hoping we continue to not show up to answer them. This leaves your children open for indoctrination into whatever way of thinking is desired. If it sounds predatory, that's because it is. And rather than hate the *predators* you should hate the *game*—another game we all consent to playing by our silence.

While laughing in our home in Kansas with his friends about what he called my *craziness*, I began to reflect deeper upon the awful battles I have had to endure to experience shame-free sex within my marriage. Sadly, I realized that I had always associated sex with adrenaline, excitement, secrecy, and non-permanence. It was a little evil. I became bored easily with men in my past. I joked about never being interested in anyone past two years. And because I was passably good-looking it was easy to change the channel on guys when I got bored, which effectively changed the channel on needing to look too deeply at myself, or my lack of understanding about sex or sexuality in my own life.

No wonder I didn't have the capacity back then to help my son see sex as an incredibly beautiful force for good when held in sacredness. Because it wasn't in my life. I didn't view it with the sacredness I should have because I had been mishandled sexually. My sexual abuse, and then my choices, equaled an understanding of *impurity*—more than *purity*. I had nothing of beauty to teach my son regarding sex or sexuality. I had only confusion. And not wanting to teach him confusion, I just kept silent and taught him nothing.

When I truly met Jesus and surrendered my life to Him, I went through a period of repentance and the breaking of soul ties. This was an amazing journey of realization and freedom, and I am so grateful for it. But all my experiences and mistakes meant practically nothing because I didn't know how to be open about them in talking to my own child about his journey with his own sexuality. I have many regrets about this. It's why I focused so intently on correcting my mistakes with my nieces. It's why they have such healthy attitudes toward sex and sexuality, having benefitted from my full understanding of my own sex and sexuality now.

What a beautiful dialogue to have with your child when it's had in purity, in the sanctity of a safe space like your own *home*. How wonderful to help them see the beauty of who and what they are and the blessing of what sex is to them in their lives. My gift from the Lord is that my son turned out so healthy. I learned many lessons late in life but just in time, it seems, for him to be course-corrected. He is incredible, and at times he still teaches me gently about my parenting. I *listen* to *him*. I *know* he listens to me. This is what *all* kids and parents need to do. Just listen to each other.

To enjoy watching them discover what is unique to them as a male or female is something you as a parent don't want to miss out on. And you certainly don't want to give the gift to someone who has no right opening that gift.

In many translations of Song of Solomon in the Bible, a powerful statement is made three times: *Do not awaken love before its time* (SoS 2:7; 3:5; 8:4). It is the essence of a warning not to arouse or awaken desires until God has brought you into the proper time with the proper person.

The truth is that we live in a culture that is telling our young people to awaken love not only *before* its time, but our society is telling them to awaken LUST. Love is not even necessary. And they're being instructed to awaken this force in childhood.

The lie, as every lie in our culture today, tells us to do the exact opposite of what God, who created us, tells us to do. This agenda perfectly serves predators who desire to see kids sexualized because of their own pedophilia attractions. No sane person would advocate the awakening of love or lust among children. Yet in our culture of lies, the push is already on to normalize and transition the word pedophile into something we can get behind as more normal— "minor-attracted persons."[6]

As reported in the *New York Post*, in Virginia, an assistant professor at Old Dominion University, Allyn Walker, "who argued it wasn't necessarily immoral for adults to be sexually attracted to kids, agreed to resign after facing intense backlash."[7] Walker was made to step down after being placed on administrative leave over his disgusting argument that "pedophiles should be referred to as 'minor-attracted persons.'"[8] The *New York Post* also noted the former professor "is transgender and uses the pronouns they/them".⁹ I can only hope the parents of this professor's students were all talking to their young people if they do not in fact embrace his views.

Wake up, America. Sick people with sick agendas are having conversations with YOUR children about having *sex* with *them* to satisfy their own twisted desires. You need to start talking—and fast! You need to start asking questions, being nosy, prying, and building a relationship with your kids that involves dialogue. Understand God's Word when you are communicating with them so you know how to point them to the cross in a relatable way.

Childhood is not the time for sex. It is the time for—*childhood.* Childhood is a time of purity and innocence. It is a time of joy in your un-knowing. We all know that for everything there is a season, but why do we let the world tell us to do things as sacred as sex out of season?

Rather than leave our kids a legacy of silence, fear, and confusion surrounding sex and sexuality, we need to educate them about how sacred sex really is and how powerful our sexuality is. We need to open the dialogue with them within the sanctity of our homes rather than leave them to the whims and beliefs of the world outside our front doors.

They need to learn about purity in a safe space so they can feel safe to ask their questions about *impurity*. It is our job and responsibility as parents to teach them that sex is incredible and incredibly sacred. As a parent, you want them to be skillful in navigating the pressures to have sex—until it is time. They need to know when the *time* is. We must *teach* them why God says the *time* is when they are *married*.

Let them push back with their reasoning and logic. Make them safe to disagree with you. But have the truth ready. Show them clearly. Lead them to a better way and save them from a million mistakes, pain, and suffering. Do your job! God will do His. His Word is sharper than any two-edged sword cutting right through to the core of your child's heart. You need only one weapon. Yet your whole suit of armor is found in Ephesians 6:10–20.

You have a sword. It's the Word of God. Use it. Now.

Many of us are stewards of incredible young people that we are raising. As young people, if you have not yet told them, then by all means tell them *today*! Tell them that they are stewards of a powerful thing called *sex* and they can create *life* from it. Or they can create death and confusion.

Explain that, for far too long, many of us have surrounded sex with fear. Tell them what you *should* know by now. Fear is an awful counselor. It is a horrible teacher. Silence from us as parents, or from them as young people, never achieves the ability to wait for love till the right time.

A nightmare never delivers someone, but a *dream* does. A *vision* does. Visions create hope, and hope delivers people safely to the other side. I so wish I had taught my son the beautiful powerful dream of sex with his future wife, rather than fear of his future because of sex. I did make sure he knew Jesus though, and my Savior has been my saving grace.

When all else fails, make sure they meet the Author of open dialogue and honest conversations. Make sure they understand the One who created them for sex and sex for them. If you do this, your silence might not be so disastrous. Mine hasn't been. I am grateful for that.

All this said, talking with your kids about sex and sexuality in an over-sexualized world where there is gender confusion, sexual confusion, identity confusion, and plain old confusion on every level makes it urgent. We have to get in front of the conversations powerfully, truthfully, with hope and reverence for sex. Do it for the beauty of your child's God-given sexuality, as well as your own.

Think about reality. The schools are saying one thing, their friends are saying one thing, the media are saying one thing, and they are experiencing entertainment that is saying and affirming all of the wrong things said.

There is nobody more powerful in your child's life than you are. If you take responsibility for your position while holding hands with the truth, you just might achieve the biblical goal of your child's saving of sex for the marriage bed. And you might just achieve this goal with balanced expectations, honest open dialogue, and the ability to overcome all challenges once he or she is finally *in* their marriage bed.

If you find yourself wondering how to do any of this, or baffled as to what they might be hearing in the culture of lies they live in at school, work, and play, then my next chapter will be helpful. Shocking, perhaps, but helpful.

I am constantly learning what else they're hearing out there in the world about sex and sexuality, and like many of you, I am constantly challenged. But I care enough to want to know and hear it all, so that the enemy of the purity I desire for my son and my nieces, and all the young people God has given me to shepherd, will not win. I know how to battle each lie because I know the truth that never fails. Ever. The enemy no longer messes with me with his lies about sex and sexuality—but I sure mess with him.

CHAPTER 11

ANSWERS IN A NUTSHELL

The Awkward Questions

So by now you may feel totally motivated to start the dialogue with your kids or the young people in your life that you love. Some may just feel that you are going to change your own life and seek purity in a new way, if not for the first time. However you are motivated, that's great. I want you to be inspired.

But where do you start? How about with a look at the most common questions and misnomers we all have about sex and sexuality? How about with the things we never want to say, or ask, or talk about? *How about the awkward stuff?*

We can't begin to navigate our way to purity without navigating our way through the lies, the myths, and the muddy waters. We have to start the dialogue—with ourselves, with our young people, and with others. There is so much that is confusing. So much that creates a way to live in the gray and avoid walking in the truth, once and for all.

We need to look at the *questions* that always seem to be lurking beneath the surface when I say something like, *"My husband courted me for four years, and we waited to have sex until we were married."* People who have already tried it before are shocked and *can't* imagine stopping. Most can't believe it. Heck, I can barely believe it, truth be told. Young people *can imagine* it but only as a *dream* they see no hope of ever achieving. Well, the dream is more than *achievable*. And more than worth it. So, what *is* the naked truth? Well, let's debunk the myths.

To dive into this, let's begin with a conversation I had with a young woman I do ministry with, Christina Boudreau. She is a leader in The Whosoevers Movement and loves seeing youth set free from bondage.

Christina is an integral part of my *Girl Club Podcast.* We live stream together weekly, with Nova Page and Christina Reynolds, two awesome singer-songwriters and powerhouse women of God. Together we interact live with our studio audience online, as well as each other. On the podcast, we often openly confront issues surrounding sex, sexuality, and God. Tune in sometime.

Being real girls and having real talk is important to me because when it comes to the real issues we all face daily, especially concerning sex and sexuality, it's critical to be fearless enough to share transparently. Millions of people see themselves inside our journeys, and they don't feel so alone in life's challenges or so different than the rest of us in what they may be struggling with.

CB, as we often call her, has a unique and raw take on the questions that preteens and teens are asking globally. The questions are way deeper than I thought. Some of the issues young people are dealing with weren't even options when we were young.

"Cyn," she began as we talked on the phone one day, "the number one question most of these kids have has to do with the amount of sexual abuse, molestation, and rape we see everywhere. They want to know, *if my purity was stolen, can it be restored?*"

The answer is YES. Absolutely yes!

For all people, please remember that in situations in which your innocence was taken, please know that it is not *your* sin. It was not *your* intention or will, and God sees you as purely as He always has. You must work to see yourself as purely also. Because you are. *Just because someone stole your sexual purity does not mean you are impure.* They are!

I am so sorry. I know what this is like, and it is heartbreaking when I consider what we all battle through to have self-esteem and live without the shame that is the legacy of sexual abuse and rape. Please *never* feel that since it's already gone, that you are no longer special, and that your body means nothing. You must change this mindset immediately, or you will continue to give yourself away. And that would then become a broken choice you are making.

CB and I discussed, "*Can purity be restored after you've willingly made mistakes?*" Yes! I am someone whose purity was restored after years of mistakes, sexual confusion, and sin.

Here's another issue we pondered: "*I have been sexually active for so long that my purity can never be restored.*" Many kids began with being sexually abused, and that has led to a life-style of broken sexuality and unsacred sex by choice.

Again, your desire to live a life of purity in mind, body, and soul is where the cleansing of your past has now begun. It is God who restores you Himself. And He does it in an instant, no matter how long you have lived the way you live. He does this through Jesus's death on the cross. To repent means to turn from sin, or the lifestyle you have been in, no matter how long, and go in the opposite direction. That direction is toward knowing God and accepting His Son as your Savior.

"If the Son sets you free, you will be free indeed" (John 8:36 NIV). If you have chosen Him, He has chosen you. He gives you beauty for ashes and washes you as white as snow when you accept Jesus as your Savior. He makes you a bride without a dirty spot or blemish to even think of. God Himself restores your purity through Jesus.

Isaiah 61 is all about what Jesus would do for you as your Savior from all the years that have been stolen from you, or that you have willingly given away. It is the very chapter in the Bible that changed my life. It became the foundation of my healing and remains so today. If you embrace the promises of the Savior that Isaiah wrote about, you will be incapable of escaping the *new you*. You will no longer see yourself as something *shameful*. Nor will you live as someone scarred by having your innocence stolen.

What about, "*How do I stop watching porn?*" CB explained that many of the young people she ministers to don't see porn as sex. "They don't get that by essentially having sex with themselves they are making their purity before Christ as His bride, a shameful thing."

The issue of pornography is one everyone, young and old, is confronting today. I will deal with it in the next chapters, but suffice it to say that porn can ruin your life and it will certainly destroy your sex life.

"Is masturbation a sin?" This is a big question because masturbation is about your *mind!* Your mind governs your body. And the thoughts you have affect the purity of your actions. Mind. Body. Soul. What thoughts are you focused on?

Some would say that masturbating without thinking of anyone else is simply having sex with yourself. You can't marry yourself, so it's essentially wrong. It makes a mockery of God's paradigm.

Others would say if you masturbated while thinking about your spouse it's fine, because your affections are set on your spouse. I disagree. The act of masturbation is usually a solo act, and that means you have excluded your partner, so it has nothing to do with your marriage. It has everything to do with your *selfishness* and your focus on yourself. It has much to do with *lust*, which we already know is a sin.

My husband was listening to Dr. Walter Martin, a former radio show host, some years ago, when someone called in to his live radio show to ask if masturbation was OK. Dr. Martin, according to my husband, simply said, "Let me say it like this. Colossians 3:17 says, 'And whatever you do in word or deed, do all in the name of the Lord Jesus, giving thanks to God the Father through Him'" (NIV).

"So," he continued, "If you can get on your knees each time you are going to masturbate and give thanks to God, in the name of Jesus, for this act of *worship* you're about to partake in, I guess you're alright."

This should answer any questions you have concerning masturbation!

Young people repeatedly ask, *"Why can't we be on an app selling sex?"*

"WHAT!" may be your initial reaction. It was certainly mine.

"Yeah, dude." CB replied. "There is this app called OnlyFans, and it's mostly teens and young people making sexual videos and selling them to adults who pay to log on to their account and watch them. Some of them do it live. And a lot of them feel it's their only way of making money."

You should be floored. I was. I had heard of OnlyFans, and nothing I heard was about *purity*. But for many young people and adults, they see it as their only way of making money. True or not true, they feel it is. Other work is available, but it may not be other work they want to do or can do. So they feel stuck.

I get feeling stuck, *but is selling your sexuality on an app really what you want to do?*

"For ratings. Did I mention that?" Christina threw in.

Yes, apparently, there are *ratings*. "*Sexual desirability*" ratings that provide *status* for those whose ratings are high.

How can you have any value or worth when you are being used, and *rated*, for a thing that is so special it's meant to be saved to create oneness with your future husband or wife?

Your sexual desirability is not a thing to be rated! It is not a thing to be *compared*. And it is most definitely not a thing to be *sold*.

Jesus paid a price for you. You can't sell what is *His*. You are an amazing being created for a purpose and with the ability to rise above any circumstances, financial or otherwise. The pursuit of purity leads you away from things like this for your own good.

When you choose purity, you choose *yourself*. Just like God has *chosen* you. You are worth *more*. If you stop measuring yourself by your sexual desirability and start looking at the development of your heart and mind, you will never lose again.

"*What should I do if I was born a boy but feel like a girl?*" While this may not seem like a question with a simple answer, let me simply ask another rhetorical question. Assuming you believe in God, *"Do you believe that God makes mistakes?"*

No, of course not. He is God. He designed and created the heavens and the earth.

Well, then ask yourself, *"How did God design humans?"*

That's explained in Genesis 1:27. God created man in His own image. "Male and female He created them" (NIV). He made man first. Then He made woman to be an equal companion to man. There is a beauty and an order to all of this. It all works to create *life.* And He wants us to have life and abundance while here.

What you may *feel* like has nothing to do with the reality of what God *did* or why He did it. When He made you a boy or a girl, He made you the way you are without mistakes, without flaws, without errors.

While *feeling* differently than what you were born to be may seem a very real situation to be in, God does not make mistakes. He is God. He can only be true to who He says He is.

The fact that you *feel* as if you are in the wrong body requires a journey to peace about your birth gender. You may not have that peace today. Truth always takes time. It takes diving into it to discover it. And it requires that you be open to that which you may not *feel.* Because, in life, the *facts* really do matter.

Truth is about facts. Feelings will push you to try to change the facts to suit your own desires to eliminate your anguish and confusion, because you don't agree with the *facts* or *feel* like following the truth. If you take this journey while walking in purity and not impurity with your Creator, the answers will come. I promise you that. And, more importantly, you will not slip and slide your way, possibly irreparably harmed, or surgically altered, to the truth of the cross and your identity in Christ.

"Did God create sex?" Yes. He designed us so that a man can make a baby with a woman. Part of His design is that we are to go forth and populate the earth. This doesn't happen in any other way except through sex between a *male* and a *female*. Every human being that has ever existed is the offspring of one man and one woman. Without this we do not exist. This is why many of us women are upset about the diminishment of our importance in allowing men to claim any parts of our sex or sexuality.

We deserve our designation as woman in our designated gender as female. I love you regardless of your *desire* to be a woman. I just acknowledge that you cannot be a woman, just as I cannot be a man.

"Is sex sacred?" Yes. It is sacred because it is an illustration and an example of our relationship with God. There is a worship aspect to sex. Just like God doesn't want you to worship or desire other gods, He also made us to not worship or desire multiple people.

Having multiple partners, like multiple gods, breaks the paradigm of our relationship with the One True Sovereign God. That is why sex is for the marriage bed only. We are in a monogamous marriage commitment to God in our relationship with Him, and His parallel on earth requires the same marriage commitment to our one true spouse.

"Are there physical and emotional impacts of sexual promiscuity?" Yes. Under the age of twenty-one, pre-marital sex results in emotional brokenness in your soul. Adults can become heartbroken by sex, but youth become broken in a different way when their view of what a marriage paradigm should be is destroyed, prior to becoming an adult.

While emotional brokenness can also create shame, guilt, anxiety, and confusion, there can be many physical impacts as well—diseases, unwanted pregnancies, and trauma when engaging with someone whose sexual behaviors are aggressive or violent, or subsequently dismissive.

"*What is fornication?*" Anything that gives you sexual gratification outside of marriage is fornication. I refer to this also as unsacred sex. In fact, phone sex and oral sex are forms of fornication if you are unmarried.

"*Are sexuality and identity the same?*" No. Not even close. One is about your behavior. The other is about who God made. God's never wrong, but your behavior certainly can be.

"*Isn't it OK to just go along with the current cultural climate?*" No, for several reasons. Chief among them, we aren't supposed to lie. Going along with a culture that is lying about what God made, and why He made it, is participating in one of the biggest lies ever in mankind.

Take the red pill! We also aren't supposed to sin against our own body, against the bodies of others, or have sex out of wedlock, according to the Bible. So going along with culture is going along with sin. If everyone starts raping and murdering people, will you go along with that too? If your best friend jumps off the roof of a building, will you follow?

Most people in our culture today are like sheep following the wrong shepherd. The shepherd of sin. Turn and run. Make new friends for yourself. Find and follow Jesus. He's the only Good Shepherd.

"*Is looking at nude photos, or nude people in videos or movies, wrong?*" Yes. Not only is it fornication, it's also a sin to look on the nudity of another. *Yet for pure sport people send photos of themselves that shouldn't be seen by anyone, except their spouse!* It blows my mind.

Even in my unmarried days, I was too smart to give anyone a nude photo of myself! Why on earth would you give anyone this kind of power to use your nakedness in any way they want? What if you have a fight or break up? Nobody but a dummy would send a nude photo of themselves to someone else.

The Bible specifically talks about *nakedness*. Your nakedness is *for your spouse*. Not for everyone else. Yet all day long we see nudity in magazines, TV shows, movies, books, billboards, ads, and music videos. It's EVERYWHERE. And everywhere it is, it's wrong. It's sold to us as "cool," just like every other lie the culture sells us. But what's cooler than the guy or girl who knows her worth and values it?

Why people love to show themselves no longer baffles me, however. I used to dress in sheer tops and embraced a post-hippie culture that didn't really live modestly. In hindsight, I did it to entice men. I did it to express a bit of rebellion because I felt I had a great body, and I owned it and controlled it. Some of that attitude was from my sexual abuse and my mistaken belief that my reclaimed sexual freedom was the freedom to give myself away and show myself if I *chose* to do so. There came a point when I became aware of God's point of view on all of this where I realized I was just *choosing sin*. It wasn't cool. I wasn't hip. I was just lost and didn't know any better.

Now that you know better, please understand this: Culture is against God. That's the naked truth. If you are going to ever have a shot of living a life of purity with its blessing of joy, happiness, and provision on every level, then you must reject culture and the impurity and lies that it's built on.

"*Is there really confusion around sexuality?*" Yes, tons of it. Just look around. When you have grown-ups saying they don't know what the definition of a woman is, you know confusion is on the throne—not God.

Those of us who have embraced the purity required for a life of happiness know one thing to be true—there is no confusion about sex or sexuality when you have submitted and surrendered to what God made you to be, think how He made you to think, and love how He made you to love.

I understand there are those of you who may feel confused inside because you don't feel the way He made you to think and feel. But we are created to live for *Him*, not for *ourselves*. You have to get your *feelings* so in love with God that they don't run your life anymore.

As 1 Corinthians 6:20 (NIV) says, "You were bought at a price. Therefore honor God with your bodies." We do not live here on earth for ourselves. We live here for God's purposes and reasons. "God is Spirit, and those who worship Him must worship in spirit and truth" (John 4:24 NKJV). Are you living a life that worships *Him*? Really? Or do you just worship yourself and whatever thing your *flesh* dictates in a moment?

The truth is what sets you free. (John 8:31–32). It's hard to be confused when you live in truth, not lies. The lies may make you *feel* freedom, or even exhilaration, for a season. But "truth" is power for a *lifetime*.

"Staying a virgin until you get married guarantees a great marriage with great sex, right?" FALSE. But it does give you a much better chance at a great marriage—with great sex!

While the goal of waiting until marriage is true and pure, the outcome is not necessarily set in stone. You can have a bad marriage for any number of reasons. Money problems and disagreements as to how to confront financial challenges or decisions are big ones. Incompatible thinking and different worldviews are also essential reasons marriages don't work.

Sex and sexuality, while important, are not the foundation of a marriage. Staying a virgin helps with your ability to be completely present and singularly focused on the one person you choose for your life partner sexually, but it doesn't guarantee great sex. You need all the other components for that—respect, trust, honor, friendship, *faith*. When shared, these are all things that create a marriage bond not easily, if ever, broken.

"*Staying a virgin until you get married is the most important thing you can do.*" FALSE. *Knowing Jesus* is the most important thing you can do. He can fix everything else because you have a relationship with Him.

If I had it to do over again, I would've stayed a virgin until I married. But I cannot say it is *the* most important thing. The most important thing you can do is to understand your *identity* as created by God. The most important thing you can do is to know how *loved* you are by Him. The most important thing you can do is understand that God created sex, and it is sacred. He created it for your enjoyment within the protected and safe space of marriage because He loves you. Knowing these things guarantees you will view your purity differently.

"*Are women responsible for men's sexual feelings of lust?*" NO. It's not our job as women to make men not experience *lust*. Men are responsible for their own sin, and to imply otherwise is to nurture a generation of pansies who don't take spiritual responsibility for themselves.

Yes, women are supposed to be modest, according to the Bible. The world wrongly says, "If you've got it, flaunt it." But what are you flaunting? Your sexuality is not something to flaunt. Sex is not something to be weaponized to create desire in anyone. It's not really about what you're wearing; it's about what your *motives* are for wearing it. Are you teasing men? Or are you dressing to feel great about yourself? I am clear in what I am asking because I did both in my past. One is great. One is wrong.

In your freedom to express your style, a man should *never* think he has permission to act inappropriately—or with *lust*. There's that word again! This is his issue to deal with in himself. And, by the way, even if you are trying to entice a man to lust, he still needs to deal with his choice to give in to something wrong. Men, stop acting like little boys. Sorry, but you have to take responsibility for yourself and your own actions, even if a woman is acting irresponsibly.

"If you've had sex outside of marriage, you're worth less than when you were a virgin." FALSE. Obviously to God you're not worth less. That would mean that every one of us was worth less because every one of us has sinned in some way.

He died for us. He died to prove how *valuable* we are to Him. So never let the sexual mistakes you've made steal your value.

I cannot deny knowing some guys truly want a virgin. They are either virgins themselves and want that purity completely in their relationship from the outset, or they simply want a girl who has not been with other guys and has saved herself for marriage.

"I need to test-drive the car before I buy it, because what if I wait, and the sex is not good?" FALSE. This is the most common question that I ever hear when I start talking about purity in terms of abstinence. People even said it to me when I was dating my now-husband. They couldn't understand how I could be so stupid as to risk not testing the sex out.

I was not a virgin. But I had decided to finally surrender this area of my life to God and trust Him with it fully. To walk in purity, I needed to walk in abstinence. On one hand I can say to you from the way a person moves, talks, or walks, that you *can* tell if you will be compatible sexually. On the other hand, there is an element of faith and trust involved here. Would God bless us with something that doesn't work well? No.

In our marriage paradigm with Jesus, we trust Him to be a great husband, and we present ourselves as a beautiful bride who waits for Him and worships Him only, no matter what. When we are told, time after time, that the paradigm between our relationship with Christ is the same one as our relationship with our spouse, *why would we think we would get something less than great sex with our spouse?*

Most things that are sexual can be worked on. Even sex that is awkward is something that can become beautiful.

"*Oral sex is not sex.*" FALSE. Premarital oral sex, as mentioned earlier, is fornication. One only needs to stop and reflect for two seconds on the fact that it's called oral . . . *SEX!*

"*Did God create sex for our pleasure and enjoyment?*" Yes and no. It goes deeper. He created sex *with* enjoyment because that's what our relationship paradigm with Him should be like. Enjoyable. Loving. Pleasurable. You don't *have* to have sex to somehow be acceptable, be thought of correctly, or valued correctly by someone, even by Him. You do not earn God's love through *performance*.

God loves and values *you*—even if you don't know *Him*. But by enjoying Him, it creates a desire for more of Him. The enjoyment of God brings us into oneness with Him—just as it should our spouse. This is why He created sex with pleasure *and* enjoyment attached.

Imagine coming together to make children and not having pleasure or enjoyment in it? There would be no kids! But those kids made with our enjoyment with our spouse bring us immeasurable pleasure. In this way, we are also taught about how God feels about us, as His kids, so we can understand what it's like to love as a parent.

Sex is something He has given to us to enjoy in a specific type of relationship for our protection and highest enjoyment of His gift.

People today are worshiping the pleasure, not the purpose, and certainly not the One who created the pleasure in the first place.

"Does God say sex should be between one man and one woman who are married?" Yes. For every beautiful lesson you will learn in this book, and every fact you will read, one thing is certain—that sex between one man and one woman who are married carries a divine blessing in ways that you will never appreciate until you come to appreciate the purity found in Him and in submitting to His will for your life.

"What is a drive-thru culture, and what does this mean?" People want intimacy and closeness without much work. I want it *fast,* and I want it *now.* And then I drive out—until I am hungry again. People want immediate gratification. Because when you don't understand that sex is sacred, you don't take the time required to engage in it correctly.

"I want to save myself for marriage, but I'm worried that doing so will prevent boys from ever wanting a relationship with me." FALSE. It'll only prevent the *wrong* boys from wanting a relationship with you. How much do you want and value what

you want for *your life*? There will always be some guys who won't want a relationship with you because they want sex now and you don't.

Some may not feel ready for the challenge, or they won't be into you enough to wait for you. Some may also not be ready for marriage, so waiting for sex will seem an impossible hurdle for them to even consider. Some may not see you as a potential wife, so if you don't want sex, what's the point? Some may not believe what you believe, in which case you should run anyway because you would be unequally yoked. *Why would you compromise what you want for someone who doesn't want the same thing?*

You don't have to be on the defensive about this beautiful choice, and if you are, it's because you see your decision to wait as a negative. It's not. It's a positive. If he doesn't see it as positive, he is not for you; he's against you.

If you are waffling, you need to get back in the Word, get some wise counsel, and strengthen your inner faith.

"*What should I do if my boyfriend/girlfriend is pressuring me for sex?*" Run quickly! Wait for someone who respects and cherishes what you—and God—want. Moreover, if you are in a manipulative, coercive, relationship, he is not operating from purity on any level. He is operating from flesh, selfishness, and impurity. I doubt he is your spouse.

He is lying, not just to you but to himself, by pressuring you to do something against what God wants for you. I am sure he has all the excuses and great lines, and you probably think that he *looooves* you and that you *looooove* him. But if he really knows Jesus, then he *knows* that this *isn't* what God wants for either of you. So he also knows that he is asking you to rebel against what you both know—and sin with him.

And if he is pressuring you because he *doesn't* know Jesus, then what are you doing?

I always interpreted pressure as something *weak* men did when they applied it to me. Because I was sexually abused as a child, I learned early that any man who is controlled by sexual desires he cannot contain, even if I have said no, is a weak man, a bad man.

You need to own your power. You need to understand your worth. You know Jesus died for you. You've heard you're worth more than all the treasure on earth, according to Jesus. I know many of you who are already Christians have heard all the stories, so what's wrong with you that you don't *believe* them? Why don't you know your value when you have been told repeatedly? Is God lying? *Or is the person who is pressuring you lying?*

"Purity sounds good, but in reality, is it possible?" YES. A lot of people *are* choosing purity. The question is, are you understanding that purity is about more than just your *body*? It is about your *mind*, your *body*, and your *soul*.

Purity is possible because of Jesus, who saves, strengthens, and helps us to be pure when we *desire* it for our lives. When you seek divine answers, you get them. Your answers are all there in the Bible. Studying it will show you the path to purity and the way to walk in it.

Planned Parenthood is one of those organizations that is very good at making the *impure* seem *pure* to people. That's what occurs in "the Matrix." One of my favorite new billboards is one of Planned Parenthood's recent advertising campaigns. It's designed to come for any of you who is confused about which pill unplugs you from "the Matrix." The billboard says, "VIRGINITY IS A SOCIAL CONSTRUCT."[1]

In all honesty, I can't help but laugh out loud every time I think about this utter joke of a billboard. *It is not even possible for man to conceive of a social construct in which God is honored, the body is respected, and sex is sacred.*

You've already seen that from the beginning of time, and all throughout history, everything man has done has been about promoting unsacred sex, and the worship of self, as the main social construct for all of us. That is the goal of "the Matrix," and it has always been the goal of "the Matrix."

This book is your red pill, should you choose to accept it! I already took mine.

CHAPTER 12

SEX WITH YOURSELF

A Bit about Porn

I preferred to avoid the issue of pornography when writing this book, but that's impossible. My desire to exclude it was because it's such a big issue to tackle for both men *and* women, and there are others who combat it daily. People like Benjamin Nolot and his organization Exodus Cry are the primary opponents in this battle, in my opinion. I support his work greatly. His film *Nefarious: Merchant of Souls* tackled sex trafficking in the most profound way I have ever seen. Another of his films, *Raised on Porn,* documents how our children are stumbling across porn on their computers and social media daily and being completely mentally destroyed. The far-reaching consequences of porn on adults is horrendous, but on young minds it is cataclysmic.

As Dillon Diaz notes in his thesis "The Pornography Pandemic: Implications, Scope and Solutions for the Church in the Post-Internet

Age," "some have called it 'the drug of the new millennium;' others, call it today's 'forbidden fruit' of choice. At this very moment, somewhere in the United States, pornography is being both produced and consumed at literally a nonstop pace, in an industry that makes more money than the combined annual revenue of Microsoft, Google, Amazon, eBay, Yahoo, Apple, and Netflix."[1]

It is sheer ignorance to not care to understand what this vice is doing to a generation. That's why this conversation needed its own section. Because it has come to occupy a huge space in any conversation about sex and sexuality today.

I believe that no person, if given an informed choice between purity and impurity, will choose porn. Yet, according to a report from Jason Carroll, "Dozens of studies have shown that men are more likely than women to view pornography, and this is particularly true of viewing pornography regularly on a daily or weekly basis."[2]

And if you think pornography will not hurt your sex life, you are *dead wrong*.

Research proves that it will. With all the confusion around sex and sexuality, pornography is on the rise and causing even more confusion about sex and sexuality.

Porn is like choosing to play with gasoline while holding a matchbook in the other hand. You cannot help but get badly burned. And you'll usually take down the whole house.

Your ability to be in a loving, committed relationship is in serious jeopardy when you watch pornography. Without your rejection of this behavior, what may seem harmless at first turns into a world of darkness. What may seem socially acceptable and laughed about will soon turn into a world of shame. *How* does this happen?

Eventually a *causal* relationship to porn, just like a causal relationship to drugs or alcohol, becomes far less than casual. And for it to stay exhilarating, you have to continually chase new highs and avoid new lows. This is how many young men, according to the film *Raised on Porn*, move from heterosexual sex to deviant sex—including pedophilia. The progression is like any other progression. It's highly addictive, so once it has you, you're in.

Did you know most serial killers watched porn? In fact, 80 percent of sex crimes are often based in porn. As Luke Gibbons noted for CBN, "The FBI said porn is found at 80 percent of the scenes of violent sex crimes, or in the homes of the offender. Police officers say that porn use is one of the most common profile traits of serial murderers and rapists."[3]

These stats are staggering, yet it amazes me that some guys will still argue that many of the women involved in porn like it. Sadly, what won't some men say—or do—to feel better about their desire for the girls needed to create the porn they love?

As reported by Gibbons, "Ted Bundy was one of America's most brutal serial killers and rapists. He admitted to 30 homicides between 1974 and 1978. The actual count is unknown and may be much higher. Bundy's crimes covered seven states. All of his victims were young women. He escaped from jail twice before finally being put to death in a Florida prison electric chair on January 24, 1989. He was 42 years old." Gibbons noted:

> The night before his death, Bundy was interviewed by Dr. James Dobson, the founder of Focus on the Family. In one segment, Bundy told Dr. Dobson about the effect his pornography addiction had on his life. "Like most other kinds of addiction," he said, "I would keep looking for more potent, more explicit, more graphic kinds of material. Like an addiction, you keep craving something which is harder,

harder, something which gives you a greater sense of excitement. Until you reach the point that pornography only goes so far . . ."

Bundy added, "I've lived in prison a long time now. I've met a lot of men who were motivated to commit violence just like me. And without exception, every one of them was deeply involved in pornography. Without question, without exception, deeply influenced and consumed by addiction to pornography."[4]

Gibbons continues:

Today, there is even more evidence of a correlation between pornography and more severe sexual crimes:
- A Michigan State Police report showed that in 41 percent of sexual assault cases, porn was viewed just prior to or during the crime.
- A University of New Hampshire study showed that the highest rape rates are in states that have high sales of porn magazines.
- Research found that adult porn was connected with each of 1,400 sexual abuse cases in Louisville, Kentucky. The majority of them were also connected with child porn.
- Other studies found that heavy use of the type of porn sold at adult bookstores matched an increased willingness to commit rape or other forced sexual acts.[5]

Gibbons asserts that a love of porn may not cause you to become a serial killer, but it's also not harmless.[6] There are many negative physical consequences to your sexual sin.

The Science of Porn: Toxic Minds

Have you heard the term "searing your conscience"?

As Jeremy Wiles shares in a Conquer Series article, "There is a part of your brain that is responsible for convicting you of wrong-doing."[7] It's a little voice inside of you that says this is wrong. We call it our conscience. "If you continue to participate in wrong behavior, you eventually become desensitized to this convicting presence. That part of your brain simply stops responding."

Wiles continues, "In effect, your conscience is seared, just as the Bible says in 1 Timothy 4:2 (NIV) 'Such teachings come through hypocritical liars, whose consciences have been seared as with a hot iron.'"[8]

Science confirms this. As Wiles writes, "Whether it be premarital sex, adultery, or viewing pornography, sexual sin alters our brain function and, when indulged in repeatedly, can lead to a seared conscience—an actual brain phenomenon that numbs us to guilt and conviction of our wrongdoing."

When porn is viewed, several things happen to the brain involving powerful hormones—two of which are Oxytocin and Vasopressin. Often called the love hormone, oxytocin is released when we hug or kiss a loved one. It regulates social interaction and sexual reproduction, playing a role in empathy, generosity, orgasm, and human bonding. Vasopressin is a hormone found in most mammals which is also used as a medication; it numbs the pain.

When we watch pornography and "act out," the sexual sin releases a powerful concoction, creating a perplexing issue for the human body. Fundamentally, the bonding hormones of Oxytocin and Vasopressin form a rewiring of the brain when consuming the wrong material, that lures the individual deeper into a prison of their own making. An intoxicating combination of hormones—intended to bring loved ones closer together and promote mental healing—are instead operating out of sinful activity, completely confusing the mind.

Dr. Doug Weiss . . . elaborates: "When [you] have a sexual experience, your brains makes these opiates which [are] four times stronger than morphine. Boom! It hits your brain, your brain lights up like a Christmas tree."[9]

I love the anecdotal visual of your brain lit up like a Christmas tree. One that catches on fire, shorts out the electricity, and burns the whole house down!

Wiles quotes Dr. Tim Jennings, who explains: "People who damage their pleasure centers in this way will often be disinterested in healthy relationships, will often become apathetic, and they will seek out either more high-risk behaviors or drugs or other types of things to stimulate the pleasure centers so they can feel this."[10]

Maybe not so shocking to some is that the Church is as statistically invested in pornography as the world around it. *Church-going people*? Yes.

According to a report from Dillon A. Diaz, "The cruel irony of the pornography crisis is this: in an alarming reversal of morality, Christians (68% of church-going males and 30% of females), whom Christ assigned to reach the lost, have instead swallowed the bait of adult filmmakers (read, traffickers) to perpetuate the industry's success."[11] A study from the National Library of Medicine notes, "Adolescents also constitute an important group of intentional online viewers of pornography with user rates in countries such as Taiwan and Sweden estimated at levels up to 59% and 96%, respectively."[12]

And, while "pornography has a long history, the new technologies have undoubtedly led it to new heights. . . . mostly in the form of video pornography, which was reported to be the most sexually arousing of all forms of explicit material."[13]

In an incredible thesis by Diaz, he notes,

With studies showing that pornography may be more addicting than heroin, viewers simultaneously and paradoxically become both the captives of sexual addiction as well as the captors and perpetrators of every abuse that occurs to people in the videos they consume, as their clicks, site visits, and memberships feed money into the pockets of sexual slavers.

Since the proliferation of the internet, pornography has become the Achilles Heel of the modernized church, upon which the strokes of the enemy cause it to stumble in the heat of the battle for the fate of the world—a problem that can only be overcome when the power of Christ meets the willingness of men and women to be changed.[14]

When the power of Christ meets the willingness of men and women to be changed!

This is the underlying war we are in today with the unsacred twisting of love, identity, sex, and sexuality. The believer is in this war. The unbeliever is in this war. On one side or the other, we are battling with our unwillingness to let go of sin and our desire for that which is killing us.

In the war of God and Satan, good and evil, purity and impurity, we can only win when we are willing to be *changed*. Sadly, the needed changes were once a normal consequence of moral people. Today they are akin to a major revolution.

If the culture you're from or the personal beliefs you hold all basically say porn is normal, then you may, like many in the Western world, find yourself pulled into the biggest lie of the sexual revolution—one so destructive that it is often associated with violence and death and is always part of the demeaning and demoralizing treatment of women and girls, amongst other things.

CHAPTER 13

THE DEVASTATION OF PORN, PART TWO

The Human Impact

P orn is destructive. It tears down those watching—and those on display. It never builds up. It doesn't build self-esteem. It doesn't build value. Anything you do that tears down and doesn't add value hinders your success in life.

No matter what you believe, the facts are what they are, and the damage porn causes is done equally to believer and unbeliever alike. To compartmentalize it some more, let's look at several things.

Impact on the Mind

We see clearly that pornography has an impact on the mind. We have discussed the actual neurological effects of oxytocin and vasopressin and how they form a rewiring of your brain with the *wrong* material.

Porn mentally distorts a person's entire view of sex, relationships, and the opposite sex. It usually presents sex as a self-centered act of pleasure, detached from love, commitment, or respect for the other person's dignity and well-being. This distortion causes unrealistic expectations and devalues the genuine intimacy and mutual respect that is part of a healthy sexual relationship within marriage.

Engaging in watching pornography fills the mind with lustful thoughts. We already know that lust is a form of desire that seeks its *own* satisfaction, without regard for the well-being of others. Jesus warns in Matthew 5:28 (NIV), "I tell you that anyone who looks at a woman lustfully has already committed adultery with her in his heart."

If you are married, your lustful thoughts are now adultery. It doesn't matter if your spouse joins you in participating or not. The sin of adultery is determined by God, and good luck explaining to Him that your spouse didn't mind.

For the believer, Scripture guides us to control our thoughts and focus on what is *pure* and *noble* (Philippians 4:8). Consuming pornographic content is in direct opposition to this principle and fills the mind with *impurity*. Calling what's going through your mind "noble" when viewing porn is laughable.

Impact on the Body

There are many schools of thought about the physical impacts of porn use to your body. Many "commonly reported problems include erectile dysfunction, delayed ejaculation, anorgasmia, and a lack of sexual desire."[1]

Simply put, your body doesn't work for you the way God created it to when you watch porn. I have personally seen marriages fail and relationships end because one partner has an appetite for porn.

Anything we choose to do outside God's plan for us is rife with issues because it is a spiritual choice *against* God and His *wisdom* for how He created all men and women to be. I know many of you look for statistics and man-made proof, but if you understand God, you will also understand that He doesn't care about man's search for proof. He, *Himself,* has given us all the *proof* we need in telling us beforehand what the negative consequences of our choices are. It's all in His Word. The decline in Christians reading His Word is directly linked to our drifting out into the abyss and having pornography and other issues surrounding sex and sexuality sitting in the pews at church.

We prove the negative consequences of going against what He says daily. Choice by choice, action by action, sin by sin, our lives are a walking manual for what doing it our way versus God's way looks like. Our way looks like *failure* because it is failure. His way looks like *victory because* His way brings us victory. It is really all this simple. And nowhere is the proof in the pudding of our lives like pornography.

It should go without saying that pornography goes against the call in 1 Corinthians 6:19–20 to honor God with our bodies. Porn disrespects the *sanctity* of the body. Our bodies are not our own. If He is on the throne over the heavens and the earth, then He is over our bodies. If He is not on the throne in your life, herein lies the problem with stepping into spiritual purity versus remaining in secular impurity. You might do one without the other, but you certainly can't do both.

Spiritual purity is critical in helping navigate all other forms of purity—mental, physical, and emotional. In a nutshell, if you are already in a lifestyle of pornography, your victory over pornography is not possible without God.

God made you. He is in you. You live at peace with His Spirit within you, or at war with it. Either way you are not your own, and the price God paid to buy you back from sin and death was with His own Son. Watching pornography doesn't honor God but instead misuses the body God gave you for sexual gratification outside of God's design. This is a slap in God's face.

As if you know better what the body should be used for? How prideful.

Pride

Honestly, as with all sin, there is much *pride* in the act of watching pornography. When we think we know better than God what our bodies and minds need and we choose to satisfy that in our own way, we say to God, "I am elevated above You on the throne in my life." This is extremely prideful.

Pride goes before a fall, or as Proverbs 16:18–19 (NIV) warns, "Pride goes before destruction, a haughty spirit before a fall. Better to be lowly in spirit along with the oppressed than to share plunder with the proud." Anyone I have known with a pornography issue usually falls in a number of ways and loses many valuable people and things from his or her life.

We live today with the consequences of the *pride* we expressed in our sexual revolution and feminist movements. As if we knew better than God. As if we were correct in rejecting the way He made men and women to behave sexually. As if His monogamous intentions needed a revision in the form of free sex (the sexual revolution) with anyone and everyone you choose. As if we knew better than God what would make us happy. As if being at home raising children and steering the future of the planet as women wasn't enough. We needed to be sexually free, have sex like men, and walk around naked to show our female empowerment (according to the feminist movement).

The proof you need is that millions of people today are unhappy, broken, and living with the pain of poor sexual choices made in moments of lust and abuse. Further proof is seen in the deviant minds that prey on victim after victim in all manner of sex crimes and in the incorrect thinking we have about sex and about sexuality today.

Porn, and the loose way we have come to view even nudity, can lead to sexual dysfunctions and problems in future marital sexual relationships if we are lacking the wisdom we need to have. Wise men and women guard their eyes, their hearts, and their minds. What does that even look like? Here's a quick story about the first time I *saw* and *experienced* what it looks like.

I was watching TV in my room one afternoon shortly after my husband and I began dating seriously. We knew God had called us to marriage. I was watching TV upstairs when he entered the room to ask me a question. He quickly turned away from the TV mid-question when he saw the TV screen. I was watching *Sex and the City*, and someone was bare-chested in this particular scene. I didn't think it was a big deal back then. In fact, someone was always doing something inappropriate on the show. It was done comically, so that made it even less of a big deal in my mind. *It's not as if they meant to be naked, right?* Wasn't it just meant to be—funny? Sigh. In hindsight, it's all so deceptive and rebellious and sad.

Roger didn't make a big deal of it. He didn't shame me for my choice. But I was instantly aware of his actions, and they were foreign to me. I laughed and said, *"Hon, it's not pornography; it's a TV show."* To which he replied. *"Babe, I don't watch anything like that. I don't want to see someone else nude. I am waiting to see you and to be forever in love with your body as you get older. How do I do that while looking at another woman nude?"*

Uhhhh, can you say speechless? That's what I was! I began processing what he said and why after he left the room. It struck me deeply because I didn't know anyone, even my Christian friends, who took this much *responsibility* to guard himself and his purity, for lack of a better word.

Fast forward to about a year later. I took him with me to see the Victoria's Secret runway show. My old girlfriend Monica was the executive producer, and while I was rather over New York parties like this, I thought Roger would enjoy it. All my girlfriends' husbands and boyfriends did, so why not? So, we went to meet a few other couples that were friends of mine.

The show started, and Roger sat through the entire fashion show with his hand over his eyes as if he had a headache. Occasionally he would turn his head or look down. Whatever he could do to *not* look at the show, he did. Every now and then he seemed to be talking to himself. I would later learn he was *praying*. Ha.

OK, at this point I was really thrown because, while he wasn't doing anything my friends would notice, he was clearly not enjoying the show the way my girlfriends' husbands and boyfriends were. This was a big-ticket VIP invite, and he looked—*miserable*!

When it ended and we were heading home later, I asked him if he had enjoyed himself. He looked at me with actual anguish and he said, *"No, not at all."* I was surprised. *"Honestly, I can live without ever going again."* He continued. *"Honey, these girls are barely twenty and twenty-one. I may only be in my forties, but I could be their father. I find it all horrible. I don't wanna sit there and watch twenty-year-old breasts and bodies when the woman I want to marry is perfectly forty. I want to grow old with your body and breasts as the only images in my mind. How am I to do that if I fill my mind with images of twenty-year-olds? It creeps me out. And it should creep every guy out who was with us."* We never went again.

My position on sex, sexuality, pornography, even nudity is so *passionate* because I have *lived* this *delusion* from every angle. I have been the girl who was proud to be OK with *all* of it. Until I met the man who was *not*—the man who actually had it all figured out, because his greatest treasure was and has always been to walk in the purity of Christ and the Word of God. The consequences of meeting someone like him have changed my life forever. I am loved the way God intended and viewed sexually the way God intended. It's a game-changer.

I unplugged yet another chord from "the Matrix" once confronted with the truth of this experience. Here was a man with a woman who knew so little about godly purity that he could've done whatever he wanted. He could have had all kinds of "freedoms."

Albeit the freedom to sin. Yet he chose the only freedoms that mattered—the ones he had in Christ.

I am calling you to this level of purity in mind, body, and soul. It is possible. I know because I got there. I did it. I saw Roger's life as a challenge, and I wanted to meet it for myself. I want you to meet the challenge for your own life.

> Don't you realize that your body is the temple of the Holy Spirit, who lives in you and was given to you by God? You do not belong to yourself. (1 Corinthians 6:19 NLT)

Impact on the Soul

Your soul is meant to be kept clean. Consuming pornography is a form of sexual immorality that defiles your mind and your body and impacts your soul. It drives a wedge between you and God, affecting your spiritual life and your relationship with Him. It creates feelings of guilt and shame. This is what sin does to your soul.

It's why Adam and Eve hid after they had eaten the apple and God encountered them in the Garden of Eden (Genesis 3:8). They were aware for the first time that they were naked, and they had shame in their nakedness. This had never happened before. Yet in their sin, they were exposed, and *aware* that they were exposed, and their reaction was to cover up and try to hide from God. Their own Father.

Guilt and shame are awful feelings that separate you from God. Even if He is right there waiting for you to return to Him and trying to love you through the guilt and shame, you will feel *separated.* It's a natural, albeit silly, reaction to not wanting God to see your behavior. Adam and Eve *hid* themselves when they realized God knew what they did. You can run, you can cover, but you cannot *hide* from God.

The wages of sin have a price. In fact, Romans 6:23 (NIV) says, "For the wages of sin is death; but the gift of God is eternal life in Jesus Christ our Lord." The death that most people experience is a death of their relationship with God. To me that is the highest price you can pay. There is no sexual pleasure or pornographic stimulation worth your *relationship* with God.

Moreover, as we discussed in the last chapter, habitual consumption of pornography can harden your heart and sear your conscience, reducing your sensitivity to sin and to the prompting of the Holy Spirit. The guilt, shame, and secrecy associated with watching pornography is something we all know is dangerous to us as believers. Engaging in activities that are against God's design for sexuality creates a spiritual rift that is difficult to return from. A lot of people who have struggled with pornography all say they had a terrible drop off in their prayer life and eventually lost their sense of spiritual peace.

Consuming pornography can also lead to the devaluation of others, seeing them as objects for your personal gratification rather than beings created in the image of God. This selfish taking will eventually have consequences you experience on an emotional level. If you have a conscience left at all, you'll experience guilt, shame, and a diminished sense of self-worth. This creates an inner turmoil that affects your soul deeply. Especially, for those actively calling themselves people of faith.

Eventually, your spiritual growth stops when you are constantly focusing on fleshly desires rather than on the things of God. The work of the Holy Spirit is blocked, and you discover that it is impossible to approach God in what He calls *sin*. A choice for impurity is a choice for sin, and a choice for sin is a choice against God and what He would have for you. Your soul suffers tremendously in the wilderness of sin.

Desensitization and Distortion of Reality

Frequent exposure to pornography can desensitize individuals to its content. Again, we have discussed how the conscience gets seared by the hormonal reactions taking place. But, this is where things really go off the rails.

In Benjamin Nolot's film *Raised on Porn*, we actually meet individuals who started out watching straight soft porn and learned to hate themselves when the chasing of new stimulation led them to *children*. Not at all thinking of themselves as the pedophiles they became, it's a sad, dark tale of how these men ended up in the worst place imaginable. Imagine the shame and guilt. Imagine the separation from anything good or pure in life when you live with the secret of needing kiddie porn to satisfy yourself?

Pornography, especially when you've become desensitized, will naturally create unrealistic expectations in relationships. Imagine the shock of the innocent woman you are dating when you begin to ask her for things you think are normal that are not, because they are normal in your secret world of porn. You will destroy any personal relationship you are in when you have learned to distort the understanding of healthy intimacy.

Addictive Patterns

Pornography is addictive. As with all addiction, you are left chasing a high that becomes harder and harder to achieve. You have to continually grow the drug in new and diverse ways to keep getting high as you become desensitized to it. This is why you learn in many scholarly studies and books on pornography that many people who get caught in its trap end up watching films with animals, films with members of the same sex, films with children, and snuff films—films that end in death, usually of a woman.

The Bible says we shouldn't even be curious about sin. Yet the rabbit hole of pornography is all about curiosity—one that can never be satisfied. As Proverbs 27:20 (NLT) says, "Just as Death and Destruction are never satisfied, so human desire is never satisfied."

Detriment to Marital Relationship

For those of you who are married, using pornography is insane—that is *if* you *value* your marriage. It will create a divide between you and your spouse. It will lead to a lack of interest in your spouse. It will impede the development of genuine intimacy with your spouse. Even if you are not yet married, all the above will happen when you are. Depending on what type of porn you are engaging in, the associated behaviors can have physical health implications, including the potential for increased risk of sexually transmitted infections.

For Christians seeking to honor God in body, mind, and spirit, refraining from pornography is an essential component of maintaining purity. It is important to seek accountability, engage with God's Word, and rely on the Holy Spirit for strength to overcome this challenge.

The negative effects of pornography can be profound and far-reaching. But it's also important to remember that God offers forgiveness and freedom from guilt and shame. Through Jesus Christ, many Christians who have struggled with pornography have found hope and healing through faith, accountability, and professional help. But you first need to admit there is a problem.

To seek purity, you have to admit to yourself that porn is an impure use of sex and sexuality and be willing to eliminate it from your life. Otherwise, you are choosing to remain in a place that is impure. Toying with impurity is the same as toying with darkness. There is no light in it. Christians and non-Christians all fail. Nobody wins. It doesn't matter what you believe. The outcomes are the same.

CHAPTER 14

SORRY, GOD.
WE DROPPED
THE BALL

The Complicity of Church
Leadership

D ear God,
We owe You an apology. Please forgive us. We have been
too busy *playing church* to really *be* the Church. We are very occu-
pied trying to *please everyone* and *offend no one*—especially sinners. We have *compromised* our way into total *ineffectiveness* in
your world today, and for this, we owe You much deeper than an
apology—we owe You our *repentance*. In the spirit of Chronicles
2:14, Father, please have *mercy* on us. *Please heal our land and
restore our nations.*

Passionately,
Your Church

If we can do all things through Christ who strengthens us, then why have we, as the huge body of believers called the *Church*, embraced the world's lack of morals and values? Whether in our minds, or in our behavior, why have we chosen to submissively blend in with the in-crowd? In the very least, why are most Christians walking around in fear of *tomorrow*—because the nation looks so bad *today*? No matter what happens—we win. *Remember*? Or is it that we fear we have been disqualified?

We show very little faith in our *minds*—or in our *actions*. And those with faith seem too busy being *in* church to be *the* Church. We all need forgiveness for what we have allowed by our *complacency*, our *success*, and our *fleshly desires*. Mind, body, and soul, we have simply been too busy *playing* church, to *be* the bright shining Church that represents a beacon in the night guiding others home to safety.

America has become lukewarm. The U.K. has become lukewarm. The Western Church, once so unabashedly bold and forward in bringing the light of Christ to the world, has lost her *first love*. We Christians once formed the hospitals. We once formed the schools. We once sent thousands of missionaries around the globe with water, food, medical supplies, and the Gospel. Now we barely tithe, we hardly give, many of our greatest leaders and movements have fallen to sexual impurity, and while everyone else screams *their* truth, we are afraid to speak up about the *Gospel*, God's very own love letter to *us*, the Church.

Even as I write, I feel the lump of tears forming in my throat. My heart is broken as my beautiful Savior gets ridiculed by those who line up to laugh at His people for their faith and their support of leaders who have *failed*, not just us—but God.

It is obvious how we did it. We allowed our faith to be impacted by our social history. Feminism and the sexual revolution polluted the mind of the Church, the body of the Church, and the soul of the Church. It did so one person at a time, one year at a time, and one TV show and song after another. *The lies of culture sit on the throne where Jesus once sat.*

Over time, our minds began thinking about other things—music, movies, TV, social media. So over time our minds began thinking differently about *God*. This opened a door for us to begin thinking differently about everything God *said*, especially about sex and sexuality.

We continue to allow our minds to be infiltrated by culture regarding *sex* and *sexuality*. *Wokeness* has poisoned many churches, while scripture teaches and has always taught us the guidelines for social justice. *Cancel culture* threatens to replace the foundation of our faith—*forgiveness*—while we sit by watching silently. I have complete disdain for so many leaders in pulpits today as I watch them abuse scripture, play word politics and church games, and seek growth, money, and fame than I ever had for secular unbelievers pursuing the same.

Why? Because we should know better.

We should know that as much as we love our brothers and sisters, and while it's not our job to judge, but to love, that *the Word* is still *the Word*, and there is no compromise in it. I don't need to name the list of sins, lifestyles, and choices we are cozying up to as normal, because we all know what sin is, according to God's Word. And to pretend otherwise is blasphemy. Let's at least acknowledge that we all are *sinners* in need of a *Savior*.

Furthermore, we should refuse compromising how we look and act to be relevant in culture. The compromise is evidence that the mind has gone into a place of acceptance of that which is against truth. Once your mind goes, your body follows. Once you are thinking differently, and living differently, your soul follows. The soul of the Church is in grave danger.

The soul is your *personality*. And, if you look at the Church in recent history, the entire personality of the Church is *different*. We were once fire-hot for Jesus in our minds, in how we lived, and in how we respected our bodies. Now we *look like* the culture around us. We often dress as inappropriately; live as inappropriately; and talk, walk, and embrace the same inappropriate media culture.

I think immediately of the shirtless photo of disgraced former Hillsong pastor Carl Lentz in baggy shorts so low his pubic hairs were practically spilling over![1] How do we embrace modesty when our young leaders are leading with sexuality in how they dress?

Sadly, when sexual brokenness is involved with *anyone*, the boundaries of right and wrong blur, and sexual energy is coming out of you from every direction. Sexually broken movements have caused sexually broken followers of those movements. Those followers of the cultural lies that dictate our relevance and appeal through inappropriate clothing will cause you to lose your position as quickly as you lose Jesus on the throne in your life. Impurity knows no sexual limitations.

Superficially, we enjoy *looking* like church. We love the *performance* of church, rather than the depth of the entire counsel of God called forth in people's lives at church. We have dropped the ball because we have beautiful buildings that are hollow shells with great music and very little Jesus. Many churches teach only enough of the Word of God to make us *feel good*, but never so much that people *feel bad*. They might not come back if they *feel bad*. So by all means, we see churches making the flock, especially the young flock, feel great—while they court a trip to Hell.

We have stopped caring for others in general, even as we have stopped caring for our own souls. Proof of that lies in our giving. According to this article from financial leader and vocal Christian Dave Ramsey, "75% to 90% of those who go to church don't give a tithe."[2] Whether you call it a tithe, or an offering, "it's not about the money—it's about the *heart*. It's about living with the attitude that we've been blessed to be a blessing. 2 Corinthians 9:7 (NIV) says, 'Each of you should give what you have decided in your heart to give, not reluctantly or under compulsion, for God loves a cheerful giver.'"[3]

Sadly, leadership is to blame for much disillusionment with supporting the Church!

According to the *New York Times*, in a nearly nine hundred-page report delivered by the attorney general of Pennsylvania, there was widespread sexual abuse of children in the Catholic Church throughout Pennsylvania and a "sophisticated" cover-up by senior church officials. "More than 300 priests were found to have abused children, at least 1,000 of them, over the course of seven decades. The report reverberated at the highest levels of the church, with the Vatican expressing 'shame and sorrow' over the findings."[4]

Shame and sorrow. These are classic banners of sexual behavior and sexuality gone awry. The result: "A Gallup poll the next year found that more than one-third of Catholics in the United States were considering leaving the faith."[5]

We have all seen the recent falls of uber-ministries and celebrity Christian leaders and pastors, like Hillsong and Brian Houston, Ravi Zacharias, Carl Lentz,[6] and more amidst allegations of sexual misconduct or abuse. And, more than ever, at this very moment, I sympathize with *all* the other *believers* out there who feel deep pain and disappointment because someone that they not only looked up to, but placed in a position of importance spiritually, is accused of a crime. I am gutted. I am heartbroken for Jesus's Church. Whether the specific accusations are true or not true, there is a problem in the hearts and minds of God's people. There is something impure that has grown and is growing.

Dear God, we owe You an apology.

Giving evidences a true *belief* in the causes your gift is intended for. It means you support something because you *believe* it's *right*. But who wants to give when compromises are revealed? Who wants to support the Church when laziness about what the *Gospel* is exists?

It seems that what much of the Church is *depending on* for its relevancy and success is culture—and *cultural approval*. Yet if that is the goal, then it seems normal that giving from believers who desire the purity of the Gospel will cease, and compromise of the Word by leaders claiming not just rockstar status, but rockstar behavior, is inevitable.

Yet I ask you this: Do you ever think you can become accepted and approved by culture with even a little Jesus in your life?

I learned the hard way you cannot. Even when I dressed somewhat inappropriately, I couldn't be *inappropriate enough*. I had just enough Jesus in me to keep me from true success in the world. Yet, I had just enough of the world in me to keep me from true success in the Kingdom of God. Lukewarm life. Lukewarm results.

I was, like millions of Christians today, living on the fence, straddling the two worlds, and not fully in either. I learned that the only thing you get straddling a fence is a pain in the groin. It is only *full surrender* to the God of purity, the Light in the darkness, the Son of God, Jesus, that brings total relief from the pain of living on the fence.

Dear God, we owe You an apology.

The Church, Christ's shining light on a hill in the darkness, is historically the most powerful force in History. We are that force. We are that light. Christianity is the greatest movement in history and the greatest social revolution to ever hit mankind. Yet, it is *us* who have dropped the ball. Not God.

We have lost the *purity* of our faith and adopted the behavior of the world because the world not only tells us that it is fine to adapt, but it also *encourages* us to adapt. We are in the Garden with the apple and a snake being enticed and seduced to blend in. With its perks and red carpets, we are in total mission drift as we thank Jesus, smoke weed, get drunk, and party with the rest of the world.

We now blend *perfectly*, even in our churches, led by a number of thirty-something-year-old pastors, or those wanting to look thirty in skinny jeans and wearing black. Blending in to chase relevance, they walk with urban swag and speak an urban language, owned by communities they have *never* visited, except perhaps for a photo op. Yet, somewhere, in all the blending in along the way, Christians walked away from the lasting power of what is right to the temporary power of what is wrong.

Somewhere along the way, many church leaders stopped preaching about abstinence, fornication, or premarital sex. Many, me included, grew up without ever receiving real instruction, direction, guidance, or understanding about things like sex and sexuality. We just fumbled in the dark figuring out things according to the information the world provided.

From the beginning of time, God has been the main preoccupation of man. Whether you believe in Him or not doesn't negate the truth that *He* is the number one conversation had, or being had, around the world daily. We discuss Him, argue about Him, fight wars over Him, and abuse others in His name. In terms of relevance, *who throughout history is more socially relevant?*

Inside most humans is a still, small *voice* that nudges us toward the questions *who am I, why am I here, who created me, and is there a God?* That voice will always be there, and as you discover, when you embrace the questions, He is real, and He alone is what the deepest parts of us cry out for. This is why *He* will *always* be the biggest discussion, and the most famous person debated, throughout your life and history. *He alone has this much power.* Who is more worthy of dressing like, talking like, and walking like than Jesus?

So, if God is this powerful, where has the Church been?

Well, I know where she is not.

In spite of all our compromising, she is *not* at the table of culture, as we would like to think. She does not speak with a voice as loud as the voices in the cultural "Matrix" speak.

Why have *we* not been discussing and answering our deepest darkest questions about sex and sexuality for ourselves? Why are we acting as if sex and sexuality are not huge issues we have to confront *right now*—in the Church?

Maybe because we have pastors and leaders struggling deeply with their own sexual and emotional issues, and opening this Pandora's box would be so messy that it's easier to avoid and leave undiscussed. I understand that. But, maybe leaving Pandora's box closed is leaving the body of Christ in a world of sexual confusion and compromise. Maybe this silence is causing us to fail.

I know *talking* about the well-reported scandals surrounding Ravi Zacharias, Matt Chandler, Doug Phillips, Jim Bakker, Bill Gothard, Chris Hill, Brian Houston, Carl Lentz, John Gray, the

Catholic Church,[7] and more is just too complicated to desire to do. But we need to talk about *why* they did what they are alleged or proven to have done. We need to understand what this insidious malignancy is that has penetrated even the Church, and we need to dialogue out loud about how to heal the brokenness caused by it. Broken people break other people. If we don't want anyone else broken, we need to confront the brokenness inside the Church and its leaders now. We need to talk about our acceptance of sin in our acceptance of culture over the cross.

But it's hard to talk about sin when it owns you. Dear God, we owe You an apology.

Our silence has produced a Church focused primarily on making its own sin seem less sinful—by talking about the gays, the lesbians, the trans, the LGBTQ people, the cheating pastors, the cheating pastors' wives, the end of our nation, abortion, socialism, Donald Trump, Joe Biden, and everyone else's sin—except our own.

I say this aware of the wakeup call needed in the Church. I have chosen to call everyone and everything out in this book to get to a place of *revival* and *revolution*—not because I feel that I am any better than any other sinner on any given Sunday, but because I have zero to lose. God already showed me that the world doesn't need another talking head on TV. It needs someone who will speak whatever He wants spoken. Once I am invited to speak, I don't expect an invitation back because truth hurts, and I come to bring a baseball bat to the heads and hearts of the Church. Wake up. NOW.

My beloved brothers and sisters, if we can stop looking at the speck in the eyes of others, especially those who are not believers, and begin to deal with the log in our own, there is hope. If we take the log out, imagine how clearly, we will see the culture of lies that *we* have embraced. If we see clearly, imagine how much wisdom we can walk in to confront the issues in people and in nations today. If only *we repent!*

> "If my people, who are called by my name, will humble themselves and pray and seek my face and turn from their wicked ways, then I will hear from heaven, and I will forgive their sin and will heal their land." (2 Chronicles 7:14 NIV)

Dear God, we owe You an apology. I know that's all you want from us to save our nations.

The flock, of which you are a part, has to stop making rockstars out of broken men and women simply because they stand on a stage and know something about the Word of God that can be delivered in a performance that is riveting.

If you take the Word, which is *sharper than any two-edged sword* (Hebrews 4:12*)* in cutting through to men's hearts, and combine it with a charismatic presentation, it's going to cause a frenzy of excitement at the prospect of its healing and promises for us all. But we don't need to be seeking a "frenzy"—we need to be seeking the *truth* of Isaiah 61 that says, "He has sent Me to heal the brokenhearted, To proclaim liberty to the captives And recovery of sight to the blind, To set at liberty those who are oppressed" (NKJV).

We are all broken and in captivity to *something.* And only Jesus can restore broken hearts so that that brokenness no longer causes you to live below your true calling and purpose. *What is your true calling and purpose?* To worship God. To live in purity in your mind, purity in your body, and purity in your soul. This would produce purity in your actions, and your actions would inspire others—rather than cause them to stumble.

The leaders whose names I have mentioned are just broken men. They come from all manner of diverse homes, backgrounds, and sin. They are gifted to preach the Gospel or any other thing they would likely choose to preach. But many are simply wounded and in need of deep healing before they get married, and certainly before they rise to prominence.

The problem is that if you *know* you are broken you have a responsibility to get off the platform quickly *and get help*. You have to recognize when your soul is in crisis, and your mind isn't acting right, and get out of the spotlight so you don't fall with the lights shining not just on you, but on *God*, whom you were called to serve and on His people who trusted you. Know this, "Not many of you should become teachers, my fellow believers, because you know that we who teach will be judged more strictly" James 3:1 (NIV). This one ought to scare you if you are a leader. It certainly scares me.

Yes, I see the many reasons why we focus on the damage done to the Church when leaders fall. It is awful. But is that an excuse for us to *leave* the Church, to stop supporting the Church, or to *stop giving* to others? Is it a reason to go live in sin ourselves? I think you know the answer to all of this is—no.

No matter what the current mission drift is that you see in the Church today, *Jesus* is the *foundation* of the Church. *Jesus* came to heal the sick. *Jesus* is the great physician. Jesus *loves* His Church. We have to leave these leaders to *Jesus* to get healed and stop expecting them to be more than the flesh and blood that they are.

We talk about pastoral restoration after a fall, but honestly, I am more interested in *flock restoration*. When mass disappointment and heartbreak occur, it is the flock that scatters. It is them who get lost and eaten by wolves when the shepherd goes down.

Maybe we have these issues because there is no foundational understanding of sex or sexuality, and what understanding there is might offend others, and we don't wish to offend?

Maybe we like the *idea* of Church and Jesus and His *love*, but we don't like the part where He says, "Therefore, 'Come out from them and be separate, says the Lord. Touch no unclean thing, and I will receive you'"(2 Corinthians 6:17 NIV).

Maybe we prefer to just go along. We don't want to be *canceled*. Perhaps we find the "in-crowd" in "the Matrix," more desirable than the in-crowd in the Kingdom of God. If not, then why have so many churches become more concerned with comfort, fun, and numbers, than the real presence of God inside?

Perhaps, all of this is because the secular rockstar mentality of pastors in pulpits today has played right into the sin of *pride*, in all of us. And *pride*, as you well know, goes before a fall.

Dear God, we owe You an apology!

CHAPTER 15

SHHHHH, WE'RE IN CHURCH

Let's Not Discuss Anything

S adly, an alarming number of pastors no longer address the elephant in their pews. What is that *elephant*? The fact that over half the congregation is in willful rebellion against God's Word on the sex issue. Porn is rampant. Sex outside wedlock is the norm. And an acceptance of gender dysphoria as an identity to be celebrated, rather than a mental illness to be treated as such, prevails. Not that the Church is responsible for the latter, but some who call themselves Christians hold these beliefs and practices, so we can no longer act like these issues are not also *our* issues. The culture of silence in the Church in confronting issues openly, and talking about them openly, is hugely to blame.

According to the Institute for Family Studies, "The GSS [General Social Survey] shows that among never-married fundamentalist adults between 2008 and 2018, 86% of females and 82% of males had at least one opposite-sex sexual partner since age 18, while 57% and 65%, respectively, had three or more. These percentages were even higher for those under 30."[1]

Our compromised stances and compromised leaders have made us silent—especially on the issue of sex and sexuality. That silence has spoken volumes while diminishing our power as the Church. We are silent because we are guilty. We are loud because we are guilty. Worse, whether silent or loud, we are using our voices incorrectly, if at all.

And worse still, we are losing sheep while condemning others. As *The Guardian* reported, "In 1972, 92% of Americans said they were Christian, Pew reported, but by 2070 that number will drop to below 50%—and the number of 'religiously unaffiliated' Americans—or 'nones' will probably outnumber those adhering to Christianity."[2]

We look like the world, full of pride, rather than the *strange and peculiar people* we are supposed to look like, as described in 1 Peter 2:9. We are often a hot mess rather than a Holy people. We are supposed to live according to a different set of rules than the ones trending in society. We are meant to be in the world—but not of it. Leaders owe a sincere apology to us all because most don't even speak up in a real way about what our *own* rules are supposed to be, much less those of society around us.

Whether you are ashamed of your own secret sin, or whether you are just afraid to discuss what's really going on isn't important anymore. If we don't use our platforms and voices to get as loud as the world, we will never be heard by the generations we are losing. Stop editing your voice. Stop allowing others to edit your voice. Speak God's wisdom no matter what.

The offered solution, as always, can no longer be to avoid discussing sex, for whatever reasons. We cannot shy away from conversations about the biblical view on the sacredness of sex and sexuality. Hiding the ball is not working. Nobody knows why we believe we are right and why trojan-horsing it across the finish line is not working. It's just an excuse to blend in with culture.

I remember being much younger and hearing gay people chant in the streets of West Hollywood, "We're here, we're queer, get used to it." I *admire* their lack of *fear*. And, because black people weren't afraid to "Say it loud, I'm black and I'm proud" in the 1960s, we eventually became accepted in mainstream conversation. Just as gays did. They used their voices and started the dialogue!

Where is the voice of the *Church*? What is our stand in culture today? Who are we? Are we *here*? Are we *proud*?

My Christian brothers and sisters in positions of power with platforms and podiums shy away from the word "sex," unless we are discussing a pastor's cheating—or talking about the sins of *those* people. Leaders in pulpits shy away from the discussions we *desperately* need to have. So much so, that we are perishing on the vine of our so-called righteousness, while the unrighteous thrive and blossom. *Why*?

Well, pertaining to sex and sexuality, I find it's partially because they are not afraid to *say* the words *sex* or *sexuality*. They are not afraid to discuss *sexuality*. As I said, their voices are louder. So their dialogue is heard. They have worked out their answers for their choices regarding sex and sexuality. They have created movements and marches and stolen history. They control the narrative surrounding something that we believe *GOD* Himself *created*. And they are ready to fill in the blanks that *we ourselves* won't address.

And, yes, there is part of an agenda that is coming for your children. And if the Church, along with parents, don't start speaking up and educating those who don't know *why* purity *matters*, they may get lost forever.

If He created sex for sacred usage, why do we remain silent, and even participate in its unsacred usage by refusing to discuss it honestly in our books, magazines, and media? Is it pride?

As the world becomes more sexualized, the Church's role in teaching and guiding its followers has become increasingly critical. We've failed to fully address the complexity of human sexuality from a biblical perspective, and we must. It's time to acknowledge not just that we have dropped the ball, but where we've dropped the ball.

Sex is a beautiful, powerful part of us to be stewarded well. The Church, unfortunately, has essentially failed to present a comprehensive, positive view of sex within the bond of marriage. By overly focusing on prohibitions and potential sin, we may have overlooked the beauty and purpose of sex as a God-given gift to married couples.

It's time we refocus on upholding God's design for sex by confronting cultural distortions, understanding the consequences of sexual sin, pursuing purity, extending grace and redemption, and equipping the next generation.

I don't expect more from the Church than in my own experience, and even I shrouded sex in fear, rather than awesomeness when in its proper place, for my budding teenage son. I get how easy it is to let *fear* be the guide rather than *freedom*.

If we are honest, I think the Church is only as good as its members, and the Church is filled with pride. Prideful sheep. Prideful shepherds. As we have discussed, many of our male leaders have their own issues surrounding sex. When the pride gets going, the issues come to fruition.

Yet, we keep elevating young men who are not dead enough in their flesh, healed of their past traumas, or mature enough in a relationship with God to be in the spotlight and leading millions. It is often the greed and selfishness of the older leaders that are to blame when they put a novice in a position to fail, for the momentary benefit of a church's finances or popularity.

> Not a novice, lest being puffed up with pride he fall into the same condemnation as the devil. (1 Timothy 3:6 NKJV)

Lifting up agenda-having, starry-eyed, immature leaders always ends in a mess for everyone involved. Whether that mess is compromise, rebellion, or sin, there is always the inevitable struggle to stay off the throne where God alone should be sitting. Which is difficult in a culture that encourages pride with every compliment and round of applause.

All the Jesus stops when the fame begins!

Let me tell you about a wonderful song called "Dying Star" by a singer-songwriter named Jason Upton. Maybe you know him? I heard his song one day while living in a gorgeous home, behind gates, in a community in California called Country Club Estates. I was getting dressed to go to a red carpet event. As I listened to the lyrics of the song given to me by my young son's basketball trainer, my entire life and all my questions about God, the Church, and *fame* became clear.

I heard this guy having a dialogue with God in which He and God work out something critical that all of us in leadership or positions of fame need to work out: He's telling God that he wants to be part of His army. God replies by telling him that He essentially sees his hypocrisy and that while he may have his best man on the front side, he always has evil on the other side. We are reminded of how we strategize blending in with the world to try to bring Jesus in when we are really making accommodations for our own flesh.

The song powerfully states a truth I needed to hear in my Hollywood world by reminding me that the only way you can be in the "Army of the Lord" is to trash your idols. Our biggest idol is—*ourselves*. We steal glory meant for the Lord—not us. It ends with a direct truth:

> But shining star I hope you see
> If the whole wide world is staring straight at you
> They can't see me.[3]

Worshiping men and living for approval from culture is idolatry. There's no room for idolatry in the Army of the Lord. There's no room for man-pleasing in the Army of the Lord. We, the Body of Christ, are the Army of the Lord. We are His Church, His Bride, and He wants no idols before Him. Not even ourselves. Not even our fears and safety nets. He wants no other gods before Him. We are completely His.

Purity is our *calling*. Anything tainted by some other desire is impure. He wants others to know *Him*. He wants others to see *His glory*. How can they meet the God of glory, if we don't get our flesh out of the way so they can SEE *Him*?

Sex and sexuality today are about pride and idolatry! We gotta tear down our idols if we want to be the Army of the Lord.

We have been busy with "man-made religiosity," as Jason sings. And if we continue to seek to rise in it and strategize everyone, and everything, all the world will see is just another dying star who thinks he or she is in the Army of the Lord.

Will the Church be that dying star?

I pray not. I pray you and I will seek a revolutionary purity that breaks pride and idolatry forever.

This song helped change my mind, my life, and my *soul*. I saw everything and everyone around me differently in an instant. I don't see fame or position any longer. I don't care about it. I care about what God wants. I care about *you*, His child, needing to hear the *truth* so your life can be better. It's time to let the world see more of Him and less of us.

The culture of lies we live in concerning sex and sexuality is about pride. It started way back when the Greeks and Romans decided they didn't need even the gods, *they themselves had created*, to justify their own sexual lusts. That pride has wanted elevation from back then. The sexual revolution, the feminist movement, the woke culture of today has all sought to feed that pride what it wants. It lives like a cancer in the Church and an ally in the world.

Even today there are some leaders who, rather than fall away while knowing they are lost, fall away while blaming Jesus for not being real.

Joshua Harris is a former evangelical Christian pastor. His 1997 book I *Kissed Dating Goodbye* laid out his ideas for a Christian approach to dating and relationships. It helped shape purity culture for many Christian millennials. He was all of twenty-one-years-old, mind you.

He has since rejected and unpublished the book, written a book called *I Survived I Kiss Dating Goodbye*, gotten a divorce, and says he is no longer a Christian.[4] So much for lifting up a novice.

I assume there are many layered and complex reasons for his departure from faith. Lawsuits, confusion in his church, the realization that broken people need healing in ways he and his former Christian pastoral colleagues were not fit to deal with, and likely just knowing what we all know—that a blanket set of *rules* for dating is not effective in a broken world.

Harris, in thinking he could write this type of manual, and us in subsequently putting him on a pedestal as the guru of sexual truth, point to the pride in all of us. Pride. There goes that word again.

Rather than discuss a desire to be pure and live like Christ, they played God by prescribing a list of *rules*. Sadly, the only list they should have written was one that taught people how to fall more in love with Christ, how to encounter Him in His word, and how to understand the entire counsel of God—not just pieces of it.

Only a push toward the cross in all things will bring about purity in *anything*. Purity is not about *man-made laws*; it's about *Spirit-made revelation*. Spiritual revelation only occurs when God's people actively seek Him for answers.

Sadly, for Harris, he apparently no longer seeks that revelation. He does not believe in Jesus and Christianity.[5] I didn't read his book in the 1990s. At that time, I was actively engaged in sex and living "sex positive" as if it was "freedom forward," so maybe Harris should have a conversation with me, because the only victory I have ever found is at the *cross*. Jesus Christ is the same yesterday, today, and forever—and so is His Word.

CHAPTER 16

THE CULTURE CLASHES

Bound for Our Sin

A s church leaders, we must openly address cultural distortions and guide believers in discerning the messages behind what the culture is really saying and doing. Churches need to create safe spaces for dialogue about these cultural influences. But how do we create these spaces if we are afraid of the words and events that belong to them?

On the other side of the spectrum, during the whole George Floyd madness in 2020, I was shocked at what the Church chose to use its voice for. Some black church leaders clammed up to the truth and started preaching a Gospel of their pain and anger against racism, rather than the one of Jesus's blood. As if the Church forgot what book it's supposed to be living by, many churches became woke and liberal and supported organizations like Black Lives Matter (BLM). They finally got loud. And it was about man-made doctrines and cultural distortions—not Jesus.

Many churches, led by black pastors, revealed the wounds they still carry from the history of slavery and racism in our nation. Those wounds, sadly, seem fresher than the Gospel. There were churches in California in the 2016 election that called themselves "Blue Churches." These blue churches were for Hillary Clinton. They hated Donald Trump so much that they chose the side that actively pushes *abortion*! Wow.

Think about the fact that our culture actually *encourages abortion*. It fights for it. It has dressed it up, glamorized it, and gotten celebrities to make it cool, even chic. *Why?* Because abortion is one of the greatest lies of culture that has ever existed. That and thinking a man can be a woman.

Abortion is simply the necessary erasure that was needed for the sexual revolution to *blossom*. Getting pregnant from all that free sex that was given to us, as our legacy to thrive in, would have been a real problem absent the advent of the birth control pill and abortion. Suddenly, in beautiful harmony, we could be sold unrestrained sex with whomever and whenever we wanted—free of some nasty little consequences called *children*.

This lack of being who we are as followers of Christ is why we are in a mess today and are dealing with broken sexuality, abortion, and sexual confusion. This is why people don't see that what the world calls *sexual freedom* is nothing more than *sexual bondage* and *spiritual chains*.

I understand all the confusion, and *yes* black lives do matter. But the Church should be living out the value of black lives *daily*. If it didn't have guilt about dropping the ball on this issue, I have to believe that so many churches could not have been co-opted away from biblical truth to doctrines created by Marxist, anti-Christian organizations.

Since we are talking culture, every phone call I received through 2020 from a white woman apologizing to me for being *white* did nothing to cause me to love them more or forgive them more. I didn't feel *relief* or *justification*. Honestly, it just made me angry.

Why? Because I don't resent what God made *you* and I don't resent what He made *me*.

What I resent is your laying your guilt and shame for what you *haven't* done to empathize with other communities—on *me*. *My* forgiveness is not what you should seek. It's God's. How many leaders are guilty of turning their churches into woke gatherings with God's Word secondary to political correctness?

I have been called an Uncle Tom, a sellout, a Trump lover, a user of my faith for money, you name it. By former friends. By family members. I have many feelings about it. But one thing nobody can ever elicit from me is *guilt*. I know what I do daily for others. I know the lives I mentor and speak into. I know my funeral will be visited by many people, white and black, male and female, whose lives have been made better because I chose to simply *love them and speak the truth*. When you live the way you should, according to scriptural love and justice, you feel no need to make *apologies* for *anything*.

If this feels like a rebuke, that's because it is. Please receive it in love. It is simply laziness that makes white people apologize for their whiteness. Do your homework on other races and get into their communities and experience what it means to *love* those who don't look like you.

Furthermore, for black people, it is simply evil to expect white people to apologize for being white. Do you dare to question—GOD?

Do any of us dare to make *His* creation apologize for the way He *Himself* made it?

Let me share with you just a bit of what God finally responded to Job after chapter upon chapter of hardship, complaining, and begging everyone—including God—for *answers* to why he was suffering so much and why he had endured so much hardship, loss, and destruction.

> Then the LORD spoke to Job out of the storm. He said:
> "Who is this that obscures my plans
> with *words without knowledge*?
>
> Brace yourself like a man;
> I will question you,
> and *you* shall answer *me*.
>
> Where were you when I laid the earth's foundation?
> Tell me if you understand."
> Job 38:1–4 (NIV, emphasis mine)

We. Don't. Understand. We need intellect, wisdom, and compassion to deal with cultural issues—especially the ones that confront sex and sexuality. We have an incredible role model to draw from. God sent His Son to show us the way. He's certainly a better role model than any Republican or Democrat I know.

Look at Jesus's interaction with the woman caught in adultery (John 8:1–11). He was a model for compassionate engagement on sensitive sexual issues. He never retreated from the *truth* in that confrontation. But He never retreated from *love* either.

While the Church does speak about the spiritual ramifications of sexual sin, we've often failed to address the emotional and physical consequences effectively. It's easy to say sin is rebellion and that if you repent, you'll be forgiven. But there are real people dealing with the real consequences of their sin out there, and they need someone to keep it real because they ain't listening otherwise.

That's why I always remind the Church that in the culture wars the emperor is naked, and we have to call it out. Boldly. We need to provide practical teachings about the potential physical repercussions of sexual sin, including STDs, unintended pregnancies, sexual dysfunction, relationship dysfunction, and gender confusion. *Before* it all occurs, preferably.

It's easy to say abortion is the sin of murder, compounding the sin of fornication in most instances. But it's even harder to embrace someone going through an unwanted pregnancy, or post-abortion, and love them back to life in a way in which they see the truth of what they did and *repent*. Repentance leads them into a changed life with changed behavior, forever. This is how communities get impacted by truth.

This is what happened at that well when Jesus told the Samaritan woman that He knew she was an adulteress. He offered her living waters of truth, with so much love and compassion, that she drank in even her own sin—which led her to repentance. She was so changed that she went back and evangelized an entire people group. The Samaritans were forever changed because the leader of our Church helped one sinner repent. He was not silent. He did not stand on protocol or wait until Sunday morning. And He certainly didn't let some other guy come along and teach her a twisted version of facts—and call it truth.

It may be hard, but we cannot avoid messy conversations and situations. People are messy, and we can't avoid people. People make up the body of Christ that He calls His Church. We can't avoid people—or the Church dies.

Does Jesus avoid the sins and awkward conversations and prayers you bring to Him daily? I doubt it. I bet He is there continuously to walk with you and talk with you and listen to you while you grow and transform and flourish.

We've all heard the saying "Satan couldn't defeat the Church—so he joined it!" Well, it's time to get real about leaders who shouldn't be leading, teachers who shouldn't be teaching, and judges who shouldn't be judging.

There's a need to discuss the emotional turmoil that results from sexual sin. Yes. There are *real* consequences, and someone needs to understand how to explain these consequences in a way that leads others away from sin, not to it. Biblical teachings such as the story of the prodigal son (Luke 15:11–32) are great and can be used to illustrate not just the *consequences* and repentance of sin, but the *allure of* it. Allure?

Yes. The allure. *Something* outside of his father's home looked appealing to that prodigal. *Something looked fun about sin.* Something looks correct, just, and even smart about sin-culture today. In fact, a life of purity often looks *boring*. There is a reality in describing how a good Christian girl like me was so ignorant of the sin I was once in, and it's that the world seemed like it was more fun than the Church. But, as I always say, that's because *"Hell always feels like Heaven when you're walking in the front door."*

Actually, the Church, when it tried to make me have fun with its dancing and ridiculous antics aimed at reaching younger people, just looked cheesy and ridiculous. There was no power in it. Why? Because the Church wasn't supposed to try and make me have fun. It was supposed to make me feel and know the *power of God.* When I felt *that* and was taught *that,* I chose the Church over the world, hands down. Purity was a logical arrival point once I entered the front door of the Church through the knowledge and power of God. Hell no longer felt like Heaven when I was walking in the front door, because I knew what Heaven was, and I recognized what Hell wasn't.

To be real about how complicated this all is, let's be real about our prodigals. That prodigal likely had a lot of fun in the beginning. They were feeling good and laughing and having a great time partying out where the wild things are. They didn't realize that Hell *always feels* like Heaven when you are walking in the front door. Always. How else would Satan deceive so many? He surely wouldn't catch anyone's eye if he came as the ugly, lying troll he really is, or if doing it didn't feel *so darn good*.

This is why the culture wars, and the lies of culture, seem so fair and just from a secular point of view. Deception is sweet. So was the apple.

In terms of sex, God made it to *feel good*. So, the best Satan can do is get you to use it in the *wrong* way. He can't take what God created to feel *good* and make it feel *bad*. He doesn't have the power to change God's *design*, no matter how hard he may try. He can't take the *sacred* and do anything, except get us to use it and view it as *unsacred*.

To keep a generation from remaining a generation of prodigals we need to call them back by showing them the beauty and joy of sex and life lived according to the truth. We must walk with them from childhood, looking at the culture around them, understanding the truth that protects and sustains them in all things. Just as parents must do this work, the Church must do this work. To achieve this, it's time to wake up and get busy talking—and being uncomfortable and feeling awkward—while interrupting the woman sitting in sin at a well minding her own business.

All the Church is doing is what most parents are doing—telling young people that fornication is sin and leaving them in fear surrounding the consequences of their sin and sexuality. We shame them before they open their mouths to reveal a struggle they may be having, so they choose not to open their mouths at all. We don't talk to *them*, and they don't talk to *us*. When the devil is in the details—we need to start talking!

The Church is the body of Christ, and the body of Christ has issues. Period. We need to stop acting like sin is outside the body, and that we in the body of Christ have all been healed already. Think for a moment about the letters Paul wrote to the Colossians and the Ephesians and just about every other tribe. Those churches were a hot mess. Sons sleeping with their fathers' wives. Adultery. All kinds of sexual immorality was taking place in the body of the Church.

We have churches calling themselves progressive. They are literally preaching a Gospel subject to their own private interpretations. Because the old-fashioned Bible-believing Church has either gone silent on the truth, in exchange for cultural favor, or mute in speaking that truth in love, wisdom, and *compassion*.

Yes, compassion. We often speak without mercy—or any interest in mercy—when we do speak. We speak without understanding—or any interest in understanding. We speak without wisdom—because there is little interest in first seeking God's deeper wisdom on issues like sex and sexuality. Noisy gongs and clanging bells are what our love sounds like. How is that possible when it's the still small voice inside your heart that radically and effectively creates in you a pure heart?

As Psalm 51:10 (NIV) pleads, "Create in me a pure heart, O God."

Point people toward the cross and do it openly, honestly, and with a pure heart. If people cannot come or tell the doctor what exactly they are sick with, how will they ever get medicine for healing? We hold the keys to the hospitals. It is time to wake up and open the doors—for real.

The importance of God's grace and forgiveness in a sick Church cannot be stressed enough. People's sin is heavy. Sexual sin is a sin against God, not just your own body. When you feel unclean and unsacred for any reason, from an impure thought life to an unsacred use of your body, the weight of it is *overwhelming*. So what is the Church doing as spiritual parents? Sometimes the Church can inadvertently promote a works-based righteousness, neglecting the powerful message of grace and redemption for those who have stumbled.

Church is meant to provide guidance and support for believers who are working through guilt and shame. It is a hospital for healing the sick. To adequately equip the next generation, we have to move from being reactive to proactive. We have to stop allowing societal norms to inform our youth about sex and sexuality and establish open conversations and solid biblical foundations for them. Church should be the safest, most mature, and loving environment of all. Church is a home that should represent the *Father* so all His prodigal children can come *home*. They want to come home.

Purity is the answer that works, but we haven't bothered to figure out how to adequately explain to our kids *why* they should be pure because we close our doors on the *conversations* that they *want* to have and the questions they *need* to ask. We close our doors because we are afraid that they will learn something that causes them to become *sinners*.

Please listen to me—they *know* what's out there. They know about sexuality, and they know about sexual confusion and grooming. Even at age thirteen they know. Trust me.

What they *want* is the skill set to confront culture from a place of love and inclusion. They want to know how to be *themselves*, as Christians, while others find themselves—free of judgment. They even will speak the truth. But they want to know if it's OK to love sinners. Even if they themselves choose *not* to sin. They are searching for how to be *pure* in this world of *impurity* and how to be *sexually free* in this culture that is telling them sexual freedom is something different than what you are telling them.

We may have dropped the ball, but we can pick it up and resume play at a higher level by returning to His design for us—and for sex. His design requires that we return to Him as people who seek to *do* what Jesus would do, *say* what Jesus would say, and *live* and *love* how Jesus would live and love.

Our kids need to know more than our fears about culture, coupled with our constant statements that Jesus is the right way, and those "other people" are going to Hell. You know why? Because they're not listening to us because we sound like *hypocrites*, and they know we are wrong in our hearts toward those "other people"—many of whom are their friends.

They love us and respect us, but they expect more from us who have tasted the power of Christ and hold the keys to a love that can unlock a generation of their *friends* from pain. They know we are wrong to preach a Jesus of love while sounding as hateful and uninterested in the pain those "other" folks are in around us. Simply because we are afraid those other people's sin will rub off on our children, our kids are withholding real conversations. And they are ticked off at us because they see how *not like Jesus* our actions are. You know who taught me this? My own son. And he is right.

If we truly want to equip a generation to counter or encounter cultural distortions, we have to engage in dialogue with them about all manner of messes, admit where we are wrong, and reach across the aisle to those who live differently and look different than us.

We must explain and show them by our actions what a bold, for the cross, loving Church actually looks like. They need to see us *change culture by our love*. Not compromise with culture by our love. *Change* culture—by our love. As the song goes, they will know we are Christians by our love. But if we never sing the song, then who will hear?

As written in Matthew 5:14 and16 (NIV), "You are the light of the world. Let your light shine before others, that they may see your good deeds and glorify your Father in heaven." The Church is and was created to be God's light on earth. Light illuminates the darkness, providing guidance, like a flashlight shines light in the darkness so we can see when we get lost. Absent the light, all there is—is darkness. It's time for us to shine brightly. The world is dark, it's true. But "He who is in you is greater than he who is in the world" 1 John 4:4 (NKJV).

The world may be a complicated place—but our light shining brightly reveals the way to walk and makes the darkness much less complicated when it is contrasted to the light of truth. I always tell people who doubt why I would commit so boldly to lifestyle Christianity, "You try it your way, and I will try it my way. I will see you at the finish line. I know I will win." If winning is what you desire, then a purity revolution is what you should seek.

CHAPTER 17

YOUR PURITY REVOLUTION

God's Design versus Yours

So here we are! We have gone through several discussions to hopefully arrive at one question: *How do I embrace this revolutionary purity?*

How do I think pure *thoughts*? How do I speak pure *words*? How do I live *purely*? OK, and let me be direct, *how on earth do I wait until I get married to have sex?*

The call to purity really is more than just an admonition against premarital sex and fornication. It really is more than just stopping watching pornography. It's more than understanding that we shouldn't be looking upon each other's nudity. These are no-brainers when you know what God says on the subject about you and your life and His plan to bless you.

We know that sexual abuse, rape, and all forms of violence are wrong and stem from impurity in the *mind*.

We know that predatory behavior in general is wrong and stems from stuff growing in the *mind*.

We know that pedophilia and desiring to have sex with children is abhorrent and wrong and stems from sickness in the *mind*.

We know that gender dysphoria is wrong, and it also is an illness in the *mind*. Sadly, we stop short of calling many other things wrong, that are also things generated in the mind, and we *shouldn't*. They grow in the mind so greatly that they root in the heart and impact the soul.

It is all about your mind. Your untransformed sin-culture mind.

This is where we are today. Hundreds of millions of God's kids are experiencing a problem that has grown in the *mind* and taken over the *body* and the *soul*. Hundreds of millions of us, more than a majority, are just *going along* blindly or willfully or *disinterestedly* with a culture of lies. For many, it becomes too difficult to impose your knowledge of right and wrong on someone else, so you just go along. Eventually, "going along" will impact your heart by hardening it or causing it to be confused about what *love* actually is. God's love, not ours. They are vastly different.

We misunderstand the concepts "love your neighbor" and "don't judge" when we think loving your neighbor means not being real about your neighbor's sin or mental illness. Truly loving your neighbor would mean you care enough to get involved and *help* your neighbor *because* you don't want him or her to die in their sin. This is why you have to speak the truth about the issues. When this delusion about what love is occurs, you stop speaking God's *truth*. Gods' truth no longer sounds like love to you; it sounds like *judgment*—when it's not.

God's offer of love precedes His eventual judgment, so how would your love not snatch your neighbor from a fire that is surely coming? Our societal notion that if we love others then we don't judge them is absurd. God loves us more than any human is capable, yet He will judge, and He does judge when we refuse Him and choose sin.

God's judgment is to Heaven or Hell. Only He can judge in this way. We cannot. But to act as if you don't see sin when you see it isn't not judging. It's being blind and silent while someone runs into a wall. You need wisdom to confront anyone on this trajectory, but God's wisdom, coupled with love and compassion, opens the door to the confrontation which should be to deliver God's loving truth.

Our *distortion* of what love is and our *misunderstanding* of judgment has progressed to our not imposing God's will on *anyone*, even *ourselves*. Eventually, God's truth will be completely watered down and irrelevant.

This is the progression in our impure world that is seeking to erase purity completely. If we stop short of truth because feelings are involved, truth will *never* exist again. That is what is so worrisome about the way society is manipulated today. This is what is so dangerous about a culture of lies surrounding impurity and sexual freedom.

Purity isn't about ceasing certain behaviors as much as it is about understanding in your mind that those behaviors are wrong. That knowledge must impact your heart. Only then does it impact your life—and the lives of those around you.

You must deeply understand *God's wisdom* for *yourself.* My constant prayer is, *Lord, teach me to think with Your wisdom, reason with Your knowledge, see with Your eyes, hear with Your ears, and love with Your heart.*

We cannot arrive at loving with God's heart until we understand *why* He would call something that seems to make someone happy *sin*.

We have to know God in His entirety to know what *love* really is, and what it looks like. *In society today, love looks like permission to do what you want, when you want, with whom you want.* In God's heart, love has rules and boundaries to protect and nurture you and to bring happiness and peace to your mind and soul. Your body willingly follows your mind and your soul.

God's love doesn't give you blanket permission to do what you want, when you want, with whom you want—because He cares about you living a healthy, happy life. He knows the end at the beginning, so He also knows what will ultimately make you happy and healthy. An element of trust is involved on your part. But an element of humility in accepting that God knows more than you do is also needed.

Your path to purity begins with understanding the journey of your own mind. It begins with your understanding the progression it can easily take away from God and His truth when you feed it with impurity.

Purity is essentially about the way your mind impacts your heart. Since we are a media-obsessed culture, think of purity as the core of a great song—or the heart of a gripping TV show. In the Bible, particularly in the New Testament, it's all about having pure intentions. Jesus is all about looking at the heart. So it's less about *"Did I do this right?"* and more about *"Why did I do this?"*

When you know your *why*, you'll easily see what to do the next time you are confronted with a similar opportunity to fail—or fly higher.

Your *thoughts* set the stage for your *actions*. Philippians 4:8 (NIV) gives us a great playlist of what to *think* about: "whatever is true, whatever is noble, whatever is right, whatever is pure, whatever is lovely, whatever is admirable." Imagine if our minds were like Spotify playlists. This verse is telling us to keep it full of chart-topping, *wholesome* tracks. Tracks, by the way, that make you feel good.

Those tracks will be the soundtrack for what you *do* when they start playing. They'll impact your mind and heart. Your actions fall in line with them. Some of you will relate. I used to have music for my *sin*. Seriously. You know what I am saying. Just like there is happy music, sad music, pump-you-up music—there is sex music. Songs that you listen to that inspire passion. If the tune is inspiring lust and impurity in any way, *change the song*.

When most people think of purity, they jump straight to the physical side of things—especially in the context of relationships. While yes, the Bible does talk about saving some things for marriage, it's also about respecting yourself and others. It's like going to a concert and respecting *everyone's* space and experience.

Have you ever listened to a song and thought, "Whoa, those *lyrics* hit deep!"? Well, purity in your *words* is like healing ointment. The words we speak can either lift someone up or tear them down. Keeping your *speech* pure means dropping kindness like hot new tracks and keeping the negativity like yesterday's one-hit wonder.

Just like I vibe with music, travel, and people, it's all about the connections. Purity in relationships means being genuine, real, and true.

Don't we all deserve genuineness, reality, and truth when we deal with each other?

Authored by God: No Designer
Wants His Designs Distorted

When Christ returns, it is called the *consummation*. The bridegroom is Christ, and He is coming to consecrate His marriage to His Bride, the Church. We are the Church. You and I are the body of believers that are the Bride that is spoken of often in the Bible. As with any other Groom, He would like His Bride to remain pure while she waits for Him.

Yet even biblical history is full of sexual sin. God denounces all of it while explaining why and showing how it's for our own protection.

He designed sex not merely for *procreation*, but also as a means of establishing deep *intimacy* and *unity* between a husband and wife. This includes *pleasure*, which is given as a blessing to keep us understanding the intimacy we have with Christ and each other. Just as we birth things together with God, we birth things together with our spouse. Him in us equals the miraculous. In Genesis 2:24 (ESV), we read, "Therefore a man shall leave his father and his mother and hold fast to his wife, and they shall become one flesh." They become *one flesh* through the act of sex. *This sacred design for sex and sexuality is the cornerstone of pursuing purity.*

As I've said, purity is often construed as merely abstaining from sexual activity outside of marriage. However, true purity extends far beyond our physical actions. It encompasses our thoughts, our hearts, and our spiritual lives. The mind, body, and soul are so intricately connected together to form the way we live and behave, that minor pollution in one area will pollute all the others.

As Matthew 5:8 (ESV) says, "Blessed are the pure in heart, for they shall see God." Purity isn't about legalism or following a set of rules. It's about those that truly want to *see* God. It's about your heart condition and seeking to have a pure heart so that you can. It's about purely, truly, deeply seeking God and seeking a holy life that pleases and honors God. *What does that mean?*

A pure heart operates with good intentions. A pure heart is kind. A pure heart is forgiving. A pure heart is loving. You *will* see God in your life if your heart is pure. I will even go so far as to say you will see God even if you often fail at being good, but you are striving with all your heart to get it right. If your *intentions* and *motives* are good, He will help and bless you. I've seen God move in my life, and I know that I often fail in my efforts to have a pure heart, but I never fail in *trying*.

God designed us to be in a certain type of love relationship with Him. Marriage is a parallel of that relationship. Your path to purity is about understanding His design for your life and for this world.

There is no way you would ever walk into a museum and repaint a Rembrandt masterpiece. You'd never knock down the wall in a home your friend built, thinking it shouldn't be there. Why? Because the home and the art have a *designer*, and you would never mess with the plans the designer has for His work of art. It's rude and ignorant. *Why then do we mess with what God designed?*

We are His work of art, created in Christ Jesus for good works (Ephesians 2:10 ESV). Specifically, to quote scripture, "we are his workmanship, created in Christ Jesus for good works, which God prepared beforehand, that we should walk in them." We should never try and redo, rethink, or reimagine what He designed to bring beauty to the world. You have a calling and a purpose. You are designed brilliantly to do exactly what He created you to do.

In respecting God's design for sex, you need to understand that you will be at odds with the culture. Culture distorts God's design for sex by regularly portraying it outside the context it was created for. Casual sex is glamorized. Pornography is glamorized. Sexualized media is prevalent and glamorized everywhere.

In fact, one would also assume from what's on TV and in our media, that God's design for Americans is that they are predominantly *not* heterosexual, that they have zero regard for monogamy and commitment or science and biology. None of this is true, but the culture is feeding us an impure diet at best; at worst, it serves lies as an appetizer, bondage and abuse as an entrée, and death as life. If we accept a scriptural foundation to understand and walk in purity, then we must admit that these cultural perceptions don't align with biblical teaching or God's design.

Scripture warns us in 1 John 2:16 (NIV), "For everything in the world—the lust of the flesh, the lust of the eyes, and the pride of life—comes not from the Father, but from the world."

God's design is completely at odds with the culture. And to lose weight in this battle we need to stop eating the wrong food. Culture's concepts of *grace* and *redemption* are non-existent. There is no grace for those who fail in our cancel culture. There is no redemptive plan that truly changes hearts in the cultural paradigm of redemption. There is no forgiveness. There is no purity.

Yet in God's design, His grace and redemption are unlimited. His forgiveness is there for those who turn from what is wrong to what is right. That is what repentance is. Turning from what is wrong to what is right, with a broken heart offered to Jesus for how mistaken you've been.

In a world that often contradicts God's design for sex and sexuality, pursuing purity can be *challenging*. It involves consciously guarding your heart, as Proverbs 4:23 (NIV) instructs, "Above all else, guard your heart, for everything you do flows from it." When your heart is aligned with God's design for you, you cannot fail, even if you stumble from time to time. Understanding that culture is after your heart, to shift you from God's design for your life to your own, should help you see a little more clearly the people and things that you need to walk away from. And trust me, you will *need Jesus* to walk away.

Renewing Your Mind: Being Accountable

My favorite scriptural teaching is found in Romans 12:2, which says that you must *be continually transformed by the renewing of your mind in Christ Jesus*. Emphasis on "in Christ Jesus." If you are renewing, relearning, and reprogramming your mind based on what the culture tells you, there is no power or transformation into anything pure. Culture will only help you transform into the image of confusion you see around you daily. It's *only* Jesus who helps you transform into God's vision for you. And, as that transformation occurs, it's *you* who can then help transform culture around you.

Our heart, and where we set our affections, directly impacts our mind. Jesus is Love. If we love at all, it's "because He first loved us" 1 John 4:19 (NIV). When our hearts are set on Him and His word, we transform from impure flesh-forward creatures into God's heavenly creations. The best way to assure you are transforming into a life of purity is to surround yourself with godly influences and engage in *accountability relationships*.

I can't say enough about accountability relationships. We need them to lose weight, stop drinking, quit drugs, have better careers, get to work on time, do our homework, and everything else in life. We as a culture believe and tout the benefits of accountability relationships all the time. Leaders, teachers, and fitness coaches all make a living selling themselves as accountability authorities.

Yet many people, Christians especially, won't get into relationships based on being spiritually accountable to anyone. I don't get it. It's like choosing to lose weight and not have a diet plan. How much will you lose without any accountability to a plan, or to a group, that you can talk through your struggles with? Not much.

It's the same with your desire to seek purity for your life. To go far, because of how you are designed, you need safeguards, and those safeguards occur when you are accountable to others. Especially others more mature than you are spiritually and others seeking the same goals.

God's grace is ever present in our journey of purity; people's grace isn't. So in finding folks to be accountable to, sadly, the Church all too often has no grace for your failings and shortcomings. They have no time for your story, complicated by your history, which may be tremendously affecting your present. Yet when *God's grace* is present, who are we as humans to deny *our* grace? *How do we transform without grace?*

Adam and Eve failed miserably in the Garden of Eden. We, like them, were not designed to fail. But when we failed, God created a saving grace for us named *Jesus*. It is awful how we refuse to give grace to those whose lives may look different than ours or whose behaviors may seem an aberration to us. We must have grace for sinners. We must also have love, time, kindness, and help for them as well. If we have all the above, then when we also tell them the truth, they won't feel the sting of our judgment—but the love of our correction.

We *have to* get involved in the messy culture around us, armed with *truth* about *His design* for others. As the Church, we need to be strong in who we are, Whose we are, and what we believe. But we cannot fear the people we see around us, as if their sin will rub off on *us*. We have to care enough, in our spiritual maturity, that our victory in Christ rubs off on *them*.

Loving Messy People: Scary but Necessary

The important thing is that we recognize in our hearts that the greatest form of purity is to love as Jesus loves. And His love includes grace while we are on our purity journey. We must extend that same grace to others.

Probably the biggest point the purity movement of many years ago missed is just that—grace. Even when we falter in our pursuit of purity, we must remember that God's love and grace are abundant. As Romans 8:1(NIV) reassures us, "Therefore, there is now no condemnation for those who are in Christ Jesus." As the Body of the Church, we need to get them in Christ Jesus in order to get them in clothing. The Holy Spirit can work with a teachable spirit. But we have to get them filled with the Holy Spirit so they are teachable.

Our failings are not the end of our purity journey. God's forgiveness is a clean slate, and each day offers a new beginning in our pursuit of a life that honors Him. I am thankful that His mercies are new every day, even if most people's are not.

Living a life of purity is a continuous journey that goes beyond avoiding certain actions. It's about embodying the Fruit of the Spirit from Galatians 5:22–23—*love, joy, peace, patience, kindness, goodness, faithfulness, gentleness, self-control*—every day! And the fruit of self-control is key when loving messy people and impacting a messy culture.

God designed us to impact culture, not to be impacted by it.

In a world saturated with sexual imagery and temptation, sometimes in our own homes because of the people who come in and out of it, seeking purity is not just a choice—but a *calling* for followers of Christ. As we navigate through this journey to understand the biblical views on sex and sexuality, the impure world we live in will continually throw temptation at us. How you armor yourself with the Word of God is critical to walking in purity and not giving in to the lust of the eyes and the flesh. By inviting the Holy Spirit to guide your decisions and your life, you can achieve true purity that keeps you out of sin, pleases God, and blesses others.

We are also meant to be atmosphere-changers. When we enter rooms, those rooms should change for the better—for everyone in them, believers and unbelievers alike. People should be drawn to the light inside us and should desire to be around us. It's not *you* they are craving, so don't let it go to your head. *It's God inside you.* It's the love of Christ that walks with you as you walk in purity. The far-reaching effects of your choice for a purity pathway are numerous. The pathway you are choosing affects everything and everyone around you. And well it should!

To embrace this calling on your life, you will have to change playgrounds and playmates, *and* you will need to be mature enough to be around those trying to navigate out of their playground into a new world of living and thinking. It's an odd combination of requirements, but requirements that are easily understood. You have to kill your own flesh to help others who are struggling and

own. You need to be actively walking
ng others whose behavior will actively
it.

arity is not for the weak of heart. It requires
ction for those who really desire to see victory in themselves and in others. But since we are talking about the Church
and its leadership, shouldn't this be the goal?

CHAPTER 18

TO BELIEVE OR NOT TO BELIEVE

Is Knowing God Critical?

You may by now be open to the idea that God created sex as a beautiful and integral part of the marital relationship. You may now understand the union of Genesis 2:24 (NIV), in which we know that marriage is "why a man leaves his father and mother and is united to his wife, and they become one flesh." You may even accept that marriage is a sacred bond and is not just physical, but emotional and spiritual. But perhaps you don't know that *sex is God's creation* and that it is inherently good, because you *don't* really *believe* in *God?*

A cultural distortion of sex exists because a cultural distortion of *God* exists!

The distortion is that either we can become gods ourselves, or God is in the backseat of the car you are driving, or *He doesn't exist at all.* Honestly, if the first two are your problem, it's because the third one is at work in your life. These are the three dominant underlying themes that culture and media feed us to distort and change our perception of sex, sexuality, and ultimately God. God, however, is *the* thing we all need to impact culture and to not be negatively impacted by it ourselves.

If you love God and believe Jesus existed, you will do what He says. Period. He is God come to earth in the flesh. And it was very clear when "Jesus answered and said to him, 'If anyone loves Me, he will keep My word; and My Father will love him, and We will come to him and make Our home with him'" (John 14:23 NKJV).

The scripture is clear. Jesus said it. But if you don't believe in Him, where do you go? What do you do? THIS is a huge question. It is one that plays greatly into this whole discussion, this entire book, and any book based on God as a source of strength to navigate life.

Believers have it easier. But even believers often live as if they believe the world around them more than God on this issue of sex and sexuality. This has to stop. If you're a believer, you need to decide to go all in—or not. Being half in and half out, trying to live for yourself and for Jesus, just doesn't work. You never reap the real rewards of absolute faith. And you hurt others trying to come to faith with your poor witness.

All In or All Out: Time to Choose

If you don't go all in on your faith, you live constantly in a zone of *doubt*, which leaves you constantly half in and half out in *your behavior*. Since our *walk* is greater than our *talk* concerning our faith, that leaves you powerless in the world and in the Kingdom of God that He has called you to.

Many feminists around the world, like Louise Perry, author of *The Case against the Sexual Revolution*, and a well-known British secular and liberal feminist, are now conceding the fact that Judeo-Christian values like monogamy, marriage, family, and commitment are much *safer* values to build life and community around than anything else.[1] Especially for women.

In several powerful interviews, in which I have had the pleasure of listening to this very bright woman speak on the topic of feminism and the sexual revolution, Louise began on the far-left side of this issue and ended further on the other right side. She now sees the intrinsic *value* in faith to achieve a purer culture surrounding sex and sexuality. And she admits that conservative, Judeo-Christian morals and values—like monogamy, commitment, family, and *faith*—have proven to provide a safer and healthier life. Nobody can argue this fact.

Perry stops short of saying it will take faith to be effectively restored, but she does think, as Heather Tomlinson noted, "that younger generations are so sick of the toxicity around sex that change *can* come through discussion and debate. She calls a return to traditional ethics 'a sexual re-enchantment process' and says that radical change 'is pushing on an open door, because it's what people feel.' For her, the issue is 'how to frame it in an ideological way . . . that de-Christianized people could accept.'"[2]

We want those who are not Christians to see the toxicity of our current attitudes toward sex and sexuality, to be sure. But, as Tomlinson wrote, "is it possible to turn back the clock without real and genuine acceptance of faith and trust in God? At the very least we need to let people know that there is an alternative to the sexual mess that we find ourselves in—and Perry's book articulates it brilliantly."[3] But is it possible to go all in on God's Word in a way that changes your life and your attitudes regarding sex and sexuality without *faith*?

I would have to say no!

In the same interview with Louise Perry, Tomlinson noted, "Rod Dreher, who is senior editor of *The American Conservative*, said he thinks we need more than persuasive arguments; only widespread conversion to Christ will have the power to change society back to one that values chastity, virtue and chivalry. '*I don't think we can get back there without a reconversion*,' he said. '*Because human sexual desire is so overwhelming, that you need to ground any sort of resistance to it—and an attempt to control it and contain it— in some sort of transcendent morality.*'"[4]

Human sexual desire is so overwhelming that absent God, as Lord of my life, I would never have been able to control it. We all need to live for something *bigger* than ourselves because when we, ourselves, are all that we live for, we do what we please when it pleases us to do so. When it doesn't please us to do so, we usually do what pleases someone else. And when we don't do what pleases someone else, we live in misery feeling unpleased and unpleasing to others and to ourselves.

Only *God* gives us the peace, confidence, and boldness to live according to His principles—while seeing the beauty of them. "The fear of the Lord is the beginning of wisdom: and the knowledge of the Holy One is understanding" (Proverbs 9:10 NIV). It will take God's wisdom to begin to understand why purity of mind, body, and soul even matter in a world and at a time when immediate sexual gratification, free of responsibility, is the norm.

Everything I have done in this book is to try and get you to make the leap to choosing *purity*. You'll need someone to save you repeatedly. You'll need help. That person you need will be your help through all of this. He is your wisdom in understanding, your confidence when walking alone, your strength in overcoming moments of great temptation, and your comfort in moving forward when you fail. And you may fail sometimes in your choice for purity, just as you may sometimes fail in your choice for *Him*.

What Louise Perry and many others ask themselves and us as believers is whether you must embrace Jesus to embrace the Judeo-Christian values He taught. They wonder if having faith and being a Christian is necessary to shifting yourself and culture out of the cesspool we are in and into the light of committed, monogamous, family-centered community.

Let me answer them all. YES!

If you want to be successful, yes. If you want to have the strength and ability to walk away from a dominant culture of unsacred sex and into a revolution that will revive your mind, your body, and your soul, yes. If you want true freedom, absolute peace, and eternal joy, yes, yes, yes.

If you can do it on your own, the commonsense results of Christianity and the Christian worldview concerning monogamy, family, and purity are evident. Go for it. But I challenge you to try and achieve what is most unachievable in the flesh without God. To unplug from this "Matrix" surrounding sex and sexuality and to fully embrace purity, you must fully understand the God behind sex and sexuality, and you will need *Jesus* to do that. In fact, a wise man once told me, if you want to know God *more*, look deeply into the face of Christ.

It's difficult to embrace anything contrary to our fleshly desires and to the grooming society provides daily without God and a rootedness in His Word. In order to get across the finish line in your choice for purity, you'll need to know God and hold His hand tightly.

Fellowship with others is important, yes. God created us for fellowship with each other. Accountability to others is important, yes. God likes accountability and order. But the help of a supernatural God, with supernatural strength, to help you as you *battle* is a whole other level of victory. Love walks with you. Love delivers you. Love strengthens you. Love wins. Jesus is the very definition of the Love you will need to understand and employ on your path to a purity revolution in your life. To enjoy monogamy and to reject a culture of unsacred sex and sexuality, you need to have faith. *Faith is God's design for you.*

CHAPTER 19

YOUR PURITY SONG

Sexual Freedom

Your purity journey should sound like a great song to you, or flow like a great trip somewhere you love that you're excited to visit. Remember that purity in the Christian sense isn't just about "saving yourself for marriage." It's way deeper than that. I think you see that it's more about the state of your heart and mind than just your physical actions.

It's like when you're jamming to your favorite tune, and you just feel that *pure* joy—no pretense, no hidden agenda, just you and the beat. You sing loud and off-key, but even that is beautiful. That's what God is aiming for with us—a genuine, unfiltered connection. A relationship. A friendship. Someone we dance and stumble through our day with. He's a parent to me, and He's my best friend. I tell Him everything because, let's face it, He knows it all anyway. He sees us with eyes that penetrate all the way through any issue.

The Bible is kinda like the OG storybook of life, love, mistakes, and comebacks. The word "purity" pops up here and there, suggesting even that the Bible is more about being pure in heart and spirit. Your heart and your spirit are like anchors in your journey of purity. If out of the overflow of the heart the mouth speaks, then what Jesus once said in Matthew 5:8 (NIV), "Blessed are the pure in heart, for they will see God," is doubly important.

You know by what you speak where your heart *is* from day to day. I can tell when there is something impure in my own heart because I can hear the words coming from my own mouth. I try to check myself when this occurs—because I want to see God. I want to be pure in heart—because I want to please God. He blesses me with life daily. And I want to bless those around me, not curse them with my anger, my sadness, my stress, or my confusion.

This doesn't mean you've got to be some kind of saint or never indulge in a Netflix binge. But pick a show to binge that won't cause impure thoughts to creep in and take over the way you see and experience life. Choose things that keep you centered on good thoughts and pure living. It's about trying to keep your motives and thoughts pure and genuine. Don't be a spiritual hypocrite. And strive to be the best version of yourself according to God's design, and nobody else's.

Also, make a deal with your eyes. And do it in prayer because it'll take prayer for this one every day. Kind of like this prayer that I love:

God, today let me turn my eyes away from looking at anything impure. Let my eyes see the beauty in the world around me, and in the people around me, no matter how broken or different they may be.

Let me appreciate what You have given me to look at. You created it, and I want to see it with Your eyes. And while you're at it, God, let me not just see with Your eyes but hear with Your ears, reason with Your knowledge, and love with Your heart.

Because music is how we worship God, let's think of purity like a classic vinyl record. Over time, it can collect some dust, and get some scratches, but with a bit of care (maybe some repentance and reflection), it can still play a beautiful tune. And just like with our lives, it's essential to do regular check-ins and clean-ups to keep things playing smoothly.

One final cool thing.

Purity isn't just a one-and-done deal. Picture it like this: You're traveling to a killer destination (let's say Paris because, c'mon, it's Paris!). But along the way, there might be detours, unexpected rain, or you might even lose your luggage (the horror!). The journey to maintaining purity is kinda like that. It's not always smooth sailing, but the point is to keep going, learn from the bumps, and enjoy the journey.

You are the owner of an incredible gift, and you get to *choose* who you give your gift to. Unwrapping it once you've freely given it will be exhilarating and beautiful, even if you once had some pain associated with it. God is faithful like that!

Sex is sacred. Sex is beautiful. Sex feels good. It is a gift from God to me—and to you. It is a gift you have to give only *once*, and then it's gone. So be cautious about how and whom you choose to give your gift to. And when you know who the recipient of your gift is because God has shown you, enjoy unwrapping it and using it together. There is much to learn, and the cherry on top of the gift is that you get to learn it with the one special person that becomes your husband or wife.

Act Now: Join the Revolution

Funny enough, the Bible never said, "Cynthia, STOP having sex." But it did set a framework for me to understand that I was worth so much *more* than "sex."

While the world around us may sway to the rhythm of the sexual revolution and cheer on its feminist beats, it's high time we drop our own chart-topper. Let's call it the "Purity Revolution." Imagine a movement where being real, raw, and radically pure isn't old-school—it's the freshest trend in town. Picture a world where our worth isn't measured by likes, swipes, or society's playlist, but by the profound depth of our souls and the genuine strength in what we believe radiates.

We've journeyed through a world that's loud with mixed messages, where the billboards scream "freedom" but deliver chains. But here's the naked truth: Purity isn't about going backward or boxing ourselves in to a list of unexplained rules and sacrifice. It's the ultimate liberation movement. The sexual revolution and the feminist movement had their moments under the spotlight, shaking up the stage and redefining norms. But they failed. The tunes we are left with sound more like a death dirge than a precious melody. Nobody is happy. Everyone is seriously confused. The dissonance is not pleasing, and the harmonies are all out of key.

It's now time for the "Purity Revolution" song that everybody has called for and never achieved because *they didn't get it.* They didn't understand us *real people.* They didn't get our issues as broken people in a broken culture well enough to know that this is a revolution that's not about suppression, but about true *expression.* Expression of our authentic selves, our deepest values, and our divine connection.

As lovers of true freedom, this revolution is one where we choose love over lust, depth over superficiality, and lasting joy over fleeting pleasure. Where we understand that our bodies, hearts, and souls aren't commodities, but *treasures*. Our expression is one in which we reveal how much we truly, madly, deeply love Jesus and desire to look like His truth—in the midst of lies.

Older people have tasted the smorgasbord offerings and are sick with addiction to its fruit. Younger people know the sexual smorgasbord in front of them is in some way toxic and thankfully are more open to abstaining from eating. But we all need to know that of all the fruit to be eaten, the one concerning sex and sexuality is the best-tasting and most profoundly filling, when eaten correctly.

The more we discuss the very naked truth about the culture of lies that has claimed sex and sexuality as freedom, the more we can freely *live*. We know when we see people who are *free*. And we know what *bondage* looks like. If culture today is living in freedom, then give us bondage. Let us be slaves to Christ.

It's high time we rally, not *against* something but *for* something: for dignity, for genuine connection, for a world where relationships aren't swiped—but deeply felt.

Purity is not a list of *rules*.

Even God didn't give us a list of rules. He gave us a *love letter* to guide us into a place of victory nobody can steal and into a freedom that craves restraint so as not to get mentally, physically, and spiritually ill.

Many reasonable voices have fairly critiqued the well-intentioned but problematic execution of the purity culture message, so I have zero intentions of giving you a set of rules. Not when God has given us an entire *book*, called the Bible, dedicated to our success in everything—especially for how to live and navigate sex and sexuality.

Former co-host of the Focus on the Family Broadcast, Dr. Juli Slattery, is a clinical psychologist, author, and the co-founder of Authentic Intimacy, a ministry dedicated to reclaiming God's design for sexuality. According to Gary Thomas, Slattery "offers a great critique that the purity culture message divided people into two groups: those who had sex before marriage and those who didn't, instead of the one group we all fit in: fallen sinners in need of God's grace. It treated *women* differently than *men*, and it made an entire theology out of one point of behavior. There are much longer critiques, but I want to make it clear that I get that there were"—and are—"legitimate problems with the purity culture message"[1] of our past.

But this is not a purity culture message. *It's a message for a Jesus culture.* It's a message for a revival of your mind and your soul that translates to a revival in your actions. It's a message of love, with the goal of "one love" for each of us.

"Unfortunately, some of those critiquing 'purity culture' sound as if the *teaching* that 'sex before marriage is wrong' was itself harmful," Thomas wrote.[2] Let me say this is dangerous and totally incorrect. *God is still right about sex before marriage.* We should wait. That message will never *harm* you, because it is not a man-made, man-prescribed message, with a list of man-made rules. It is God's message. To you. Whether or not you even know Him.

The problem is that man tried to take a God-message that needed to be spoken by God to us individually, and written on our hearts individually, and make it his own. Man tried to write a prescription for sex and sexuality, when all we have ever needed to do is point people to the cross, and then walk with them over the bridge from the world to the Kingdom. But that takes time, work—and love. And perhaps some psychologists, therapists, and doctors!

Louise Perry, the British writer I quoted earlier, offers a refreshing bridge for the *unbeliever* to walk across.

But please be clear that the ultimate victory, on the other side of that bridge, does end in a place of waiting for sex until you are married. I know this because I have also walked across the bridge called faith.

As Thomas noted, "Rather than citing Scripture, [Perry] cites consequences and studies (which makes sense for her purposes)"[3] and to be honest, it makes sense even for us as Christians to see the real facts and consequences of a choice to continue in impurity. I found her book to be a brilliant and much-needed read for anyone who promotes or unwittingly accepts the destruction sold to us in the "hook-up" culture message.

By now I hope you fully get that we are not able to go forward with any of the religiosity and bondage the Church once used, nor are we able to go forward in this "free for all" "do what thou will" ode to satanism form of bondage either.

So, grab your metaphorical mics, and embrace a new song, as you step into the light. Let's start a new movement—one that shouts for purity, not out of fear, but out of fierce, bold *love*.

The spotlight's on you now. You have the information. You have the choice. Will you remain silent, or just dance to the tune everyone else is jamming to, or will you be the game-changer who sparks a new beat for yourself and those around you?

We are all called to lead those around us. It may sound impossible—but the world around you is truly waiting for you to be who God created you to be, because the best leadership occurs by example.

The call to action is clear: *Let's redefine cool.*

Let's make purity the new musical anthem for our generation. God has sung a song over you from day one. It is a song of purity, love, and freedom. It is a song that celebrates His gift of sex and the sacredness of how you experience it. With Him, you have the strength to sing this new song over your life—and the lives of others.

Deep down, we all know the naked truth is that we have been sold a number of cultural lies.

But we know what Jesus meant when He told us, "Don't copy the behavior and customs of this world, but let God transform you into a new person by changing the way you think. Then you will learn to know God's will for you, which is good and pleasing and perfect" (Romans 12:2 NLT).

This transformation is the melody that creates the most beautiful song you can experience for your own happiness and the happiness of others.

It's time, my friends. For many years I struggled to compose this song about purity. For many years I felt an inner revolution grow inside me. It's time to set *your* mind free and feel your soul smile, as your body follows the inner revolution inside of you too.

It's time to sing your new song. And make it the boldest song you've ever sung.

Are you with me?

For more information, please visit www.cynthiagarrett.org.

ACKNOWLEDGMENTS

Special Thanks to Anna Richards . . . for everything, every day, all the time!

Special thanks to my husband, my son Christian, my niece Summer, and my bonus son Mario for bearing with my disappearing from holidays and family gatherings for over two years to write this book!

Special thanks to the women of Cynthia Garrett's Girl Club who join me weekly in sharing their journeys so that others learn to embrace a life of purity—mind, body, and soul.

ENDNOTES

Introduction

1 Sarah Melancon, Ph.D., "Frequency of Sex before Marriage: Statistics & Trends," Women's Health Interactive, November 2023, https://www.womens-health.com/sex-before-marriage -statistics#:~:text=Frequency%20Of%20Sex%20Before%20 Marriage%3A%20Statistics%20%26%20Trends,public%20 views%20it%20as%20acceptable.&text=Written%20%26%20 Fact%2DChecked%20By%3A,Sarah%20Melancon%2C%20Ph.

2 Jeff Diamant, "Half of U.S. Christians Say Casual Sex between Consenting Adults Is Sometimes or Always Acceptable," Pew Research Center, August 31, 2020, https://www.pewresearch .org/short-reads/2020/08/31/half-of-u-s-christians-say-casual-sex -between-consenting-adults-is-sometimes-or-always-acceptable/.

CHAPTER 1: Unveiling the Past

1 Anne-Marie Slaughter, "Why Women Still Can't Have It All," *The Atlantic*, July/August 2012 Issue, https://www.theatlantic.com/magazine/archive/2012/07/why-women-still-cant-have-it-all/309020/.

2 Ibid.

3 Ibid

CHAPTER 2: The Damaged Self

1 Claire McNear, "'Too Hot to Handle' Is Netflix's Most Disconcerting, and Entertaining, Reality TV Show Yet," The Ringer, April 17, 2020, https://www.theringer.com/tv/2020/4/17/21224988/too-hot-to-handle-netflix-reality-tv-show.

2 Ibid.

3 Ibid.

4 Elizabeth Wildsmith, Jennifer Manlove, and Elizabeth Cook, "Dramatic Increase in the Proportion of Births outside of Marriage in the United States from 1990 to 2016," Child Trends, August 8, 2018, https://www.childtrends.org/publications/dramatic-increase-in-percentage-of-births-outside-marriage-among-whites-hispanics-and-women-with-higher-education-levels#.

5 Roland von Känel, Sonja Weilenmann, and Tobias R. Spiller, "Loneliness Is Associated with Depressive Affect, but Not with Most Other Symptoms of Depression in Community-Dwelling Individuals: A Network Analysis," National Library of Medicine, March 18, 2021, https://www.ncbi.nlm.nih.gov/pmc/articles/PMC7967763/#:~:text=The%20prevalence%20of%20loneliness%20(sometimes,0.001)%2C%20independent%20of%20covariates.

Endnotes

CHAPTER 4: Consent

1 Walter Isaacson, "Inside Elon Musk's Struggle for the Future of AI," *Time Magazine*, September 6, 2023, https://time.com/6310076/elon-musk-ai-walter-isaacson-biography/.

2 Lee Brown, "Embattled Balenciaga Seeking Crisis Management Expert after BDSM Ad," *New York Post*, March 1, 2023, https://nypost.com/2023/03/01/balenciaga-seeks-crisis-management-expert-after-bdsm-ad-scandal/.

3 Andrea Felsted, "The Bud Light Hangover Hasn't Gone Away," *Bloomberg*, August 3, 2023, https://www.bloomberg.com/opinion/articles/2023-08-03/ab-inbev-s-bud-light-controversy-hasn-t-faded-and-people-are-drinking-less-beer.

4 Ronny Reyes, "Target Loses $10B in 10 Days as Stocks Fall Following Boycott over LGBTQ-Friendly Kids Clothing," *New York Post*, May 28, 2023, https://nypost.com/2023/05/28/target-loses-10b-following-boycott-calls-over-lgbtq-friendly-clothing/; and Janay Kingsberry, "Trans Designer Dumped by Target Explains How He Got Smeared as Satanist," the *Washington Post*, May 26, 2023, https://www.washingtonpost.com/lifestyle/2023/05/26/lgbtq-designer-target-pride-collection-controversy/.

5 See https://www.2ndvote.com/.

6 Hamza Shaban, "Target and Bud Light Become Cautionary Tales after Political Boycotts," Yahoo Finance, August 17, 2023, https://finance.yahoo.com/news/target-and-bud-light-become-cautionary-tales-after-political-boycotts-093020210.html?guccounter=1&guce_referrer=aHR0cHM6Ly93d3cuZ29vZ2xlLmNvbS8&guce_referrer_sig=AQAAAJKmWMyIMV-TiFVb6tqBL773WZHp1s0J73puEXJ5ZftKKvcLoTJ_kpC0INahtybSplt-mINwXzZqH5P4qDOS6Hl53S

267

WaR6N0bfhbt1dWPlsZBbL9Re7Zt1WwX-gePWnEAHr
-NoQIsLwE0nElNzd1oBUQg2xLDk_IMDMo6odu6vx2.

7   Kayla Kuefler, "Love at First Swipe: The Evolution of Online
    Dating," Stylight, 2019, https://www.stylight.com/Magazine
    /Lifestyle/Love-First-Swipe-Evolution-Online-Dating/.

8   Ibid.

9   "Social Media Fact Sheet," Pew Research Center, April 7, 2021,
    https://www.pewresearch.org/internet/fact-sheet/social-media/.

10 Andrew Perrin, Sara Arske, "About Three-in-Ten U.S. Adults
    Say They Are 'Almost Constantly' Online," Pew Research
    Center, March 26, 2023, https://www.pewresearch.org/short
    -reads/2021/03/26/about-three-in-ten-u-s-adults-say-they-are
    -almost-constantly-online/.

11 Kuefler, "Love at First Swipe."

12 Ibid.

13 Ibid.

CHAPTER 8: Saying "I Do" When You Already Did

1   Nicholas H. Wolfinger, "Does Sexual History Affect Marital
    Happiness?," Institute for Family Studies, October 22, 2018,
    https://ifstudies.org/blog/does-sexual-history-affect-marital
    -happiness.

2   Olga Khazan, "Fewer Sex Partners Means a Happier Marriage,"
    The Atlantic, October 22, 2018, https://www.theatlantic.com
    /health/archive/2018/10/sexual-partners-and-marital-happiness
    /573493/.

3   Jay Teachman, "Premarital Sex, Premarital Cohabitation, and the
    Risk of Subsequent Marital Dissolution Among Women," *Journal*

of Marriage and Family, Vol. 65, Issue 2, May 2003, pages 444-55, https://onlinelibrary.wiley.com/doi/abs/10.1111/j.1741-3737 .2003.00444.x.

4   HD Retro Trailers, "*The Blue Lagoon* (1980) ORIGINAL TRAILER [HD 1080p]," YouTube, https://www.youtube.com /watch?v=A0UapwJIJn8.

CHAPTER 9: Identity

1   See Walt Heyer, "Sex Change Regret," https://sexchangeregret.com/.
2   Abigail Shrier, *Irreversible Damage: The Transgender Craze Seducing Our Daughters* (Washington, DC: Regnery Publishing, 2020),127.

CHAPTER 10: If You Aren't Talking, Who Is?

1   John Matarazzo, "Pastor Reads Explicit Children's Book at School Board Meeting - Sparks Controversy!," Charisma News, May 25, 2023, https://www.youtube.com/watch?v=bdmR-n0zlUg.
2   Bailee Hill, "North Carolina Pastor Eviscerates 'Woke' School Board for 'Perverted' Library Book: 'This Is Sinister,'" Fox News, May 18, 2023, https://www.foxnews.com/media/north-carolina -pastor-eviscerates-woke-school-board-perverted-library-book -sinister.
3   America Reports, "Missouri Teacher who Resigned after School Found out about Her OnlyFans Says She's Made Close to $1 Million," Fox News, October 19, 2023, https://www.foxnews .com/video/6339481305112.
4   Ronny Reyes, "Oregon HS Students Had to Write 'Sexual Fantasy,' Include Sex Toys in Assignment," *New York Post*, March 14, 2023, https://nypost.com/2023/03/14/oregon-hs-class-had -to-write-sexual-fantasy-include-sex-toys/.

5   Susannah Luthi, "XXXtra Credit: Oregon Teacher Asks Students
    to Describe Erotic Fantasies and Identify Sexually Attractive
    Classmates," *Washington Free Beacon*, March 14, 2023,
    https://freebeacon.com/campus/xxxtra-credit-oregon-teacher
    -asks-students-to-describe-erotic-fantasies-and-identify-sexually
    -attractive-classmates/.

6   Jo Bartosch, "'Minor-Attracted People' Is an Attempt to Sanitise
    Child Abuse," Spiked, January 3, 2023, https://www.spiked
    -online.com/2023/01/03/minor-attracted-people-is-an-attempt
    -to-sanitise-child-abuse/.

7   Emily Crane, "Prof Who Said Pedophiles Should Be Called
    'Minor-Attracted Persons' Agrees to Resign," *New York Post*,
    November 25, 2021, https://nypost.com/2021/11/25/prof-who
    -referred-to-pedophiles-as-minor-attracted-persons-to-resign/.

8   Ibid.

9   Ibid.

CHAPTER 11: Answers in a Nutshell

1   Planned Parenthood, "Virginity is a social construct," X (formerly
    Twitter), June 29, 2023, https://twitter.com/PPFA/status
    /1674462837425446912.

CHAPTER 12: Sex with Yourself

1   Dillon A. Diaz, "The Pornography Pandemic: Implications,
    Scope and Solutions for the Church in the Post-Internet Age,"
    Southeastern University FireScholars, Spring 2018, https://
    firescholars.seu.edu/cgi/viewcontent.cgi?article=1127&context
    =honors.

2   Jason Carroll, "Porn Gap: Difference in Men and Women
    Pornography Patterns," Wheatley Institute, April 18, 2023,

https://wheatley.byu.edu/family/porn-gap-difference-in-men
-and-women-pornography-patterns#:~:text=Dozens%20of%20
studies%20have%20shown,a%20daily%20or%20weekly%20
basis.

3 Luke Gibbons, "Serial Killer Ted Bundy Describes the Dangers of
Pornography," CBN, October 31, 2018, https://www2.cbn.com
/news/us/serial-killer-ted-bundy-describes-dangers-pornography.

4 Ibid.

5 Ibid.

6 Ibid

7 Jeremy Wiles, "Why Is Sexual Sin Against Your Own Body?,"
Conquer Series, April 26, 2022, https://conquerseries.com/why
-sexual-sin-against-your-body.

8 Ibid.

9 Ibid.

10 Ibid.

11 Dillon A. Diaz, "The Pornography Pandemic: Implications,
Scope and Solutions for the Church in the Post-Internet Age,"
Southeastern University FireScholars, Spring 2018, https://
firescholars.seu.edu/cgi/viewcontent.cgi?article=1127&context
=honors.

12 Aleksandra Diana Dwulit and Piotr Rzymski, "Prevalence, Patterns
and Self-Perceived Effects of Pornography Consumption in Polish
University Students: A Cross-Sectional Study," National Library
of Medicine, May 27, 2019, https://www.ncbi.nlm.nih.gov/pmc
/articles/PMC6571756/.

13 Ibid.

14 Diaz, "The Pornography Pandemic."

CHAPTER 13: The Devastation of Porn, Part Two

1 Wikipedia Community, "Effects of Pornography," Wikipedia, page last updated December 3, 2023, https://en.wikipedia.org/wiki/Effects_of_pornography#:~:text=Sexual%20function%20is%20a%20rising,a%20lack%20of%20sexual%20desire.

CHAPTER 14: Sorry, God. We Dropped the Ball

1 Kyle Kiningham, "The Dick Root Always Tells the Truth," Medium, January 27, 2021, https://medium.com/@hxiwbyvebx/carl-lentzs-true-tell-cbad200ccd5c.

2 Ramsey Solutions, "Tithes and Offerings: Your Questions Answered," Ramsey Solutions, August 29, 2023, https://www.ramseysolutions.com/budgeting/daves-advice-on-tithing-and-giving#:~:text=God%20loves%20us%20when%20we,don%27t%20give%20a%20tithe.

3 Ibid.

4 Ruth Graham, "What the Latest Investigations into Catholic Church Sex Abuse Mean," *New York Times*, June 2, 2023, https://www.nytimes.com/2023/06/02/us/catholic-church-sex-abuse-investigations.html#:~:text=More%20than%20300%20priests%20were,and%20sorrow"%20over%20the%20findings.

5 Ibid.

6 David Smith, "'Why Do Pastors Keep Falling?': Inside the Shocking Downfall of Hillsong Church," *The Guardian*, May 18 2023, https://www.theguardian.com/tv-and-radio/2023/may/18/hillsong-church-documentary-carl-lentz-scandal; Ruth Graham, "Ravi Zacharias, Influential Evangelist, Is Accused of Sexual Abuse in Scathing Report," *New York Times*, February 11, 2021, https://www.nytimes.com/2021/02/11/us/ravi-zacharias-sexual-abuse.

html; Tracy Wright, "Disgraced Celebrity Pastor Carl Lentz
Cheated with Family Nanny; Hillsong Church Documentary
Details Scandal," Fox News, May 15 2023, https://www.foxnews
.com/entertainment/disgraced-celebrity-pastor-carl-lentz-cheated
-family-nanny-hillsong-church-documentary-details-scandal.

7 Ruth Graham, "Ravi Zacharias, Influential Evangelist, Is Accused
   of Sexual Abuse in Scathing Report," *New York Times*,
   February 11, 2021, https://www.nytimes.com/2021/02/11/us/ravi
   -zacharias-sexual-abuse.html; Vanessa Serna, "Married Pastor, 48,
   Takes Leave of Absence over 'Coarse' Messages with Woman Who
   Wasn't His Wife - but Church Says the Texts WEREN'T Sexual,"
   Daily Mail, August 30, 2022, https://www.dailymail.co.uk
   /news/article-11162041/Married-Texas-pastor-tells-congregation
   -stepping-amid-cheating-scandal.html; David McCormack,
   "Leader of Christian Ministry Followed by the Duggar Family
   from TLC's 19 Kids and Counting Is Accused of Using Teenage
   Girl as 'Personal Sex Slave' in $1m Lawsuit," *Daily Mail*,
   April 17, 2014, https://www.dailymail.co.uk/news/article
   -2606528/Leader-Christian-ministry-followed-Duggar-family
   -TLCs-19-Kids-And-Counting-accused-using-teenage-girl
   -personal-sex-slave-1m-lawsuit.html; Lauren Effron, Andrew
   Paparella, and Jeca Taudte, "The Scandals that Brought down the
   Bakkers, Once among US's Most Famous Televangelists," ABC
   News, December 20, 2019, https://abcnews.go.com/US/scandals
   -brought-bakkers-uss-famous-televangelists/story?id=60389342;
   Sarah Pulliam Bailey, "New Charges Allege Religious Leader, Who
   Has Ties to the Duggars, Sexually Abused Women," *Washington
   Post*, January 6, 2016, https://www.washingtonpost
   .com/news/acts-of-faith/wp/2016/01/06/new-charges-allege
   -religious-leader-who-has-ties-to-the-duggars-sexually-abused

-women/; Leonardo Blair, "Potter's House Denver Pastor Chris Hill Resigns over Alleged Affair, Separates From Wife," *Christian Post*, April 25, 2017, https://www.christianpost.com /news/potters-house-denver-pastor-chris-hill-resigns-over-alleged -affair-separates-from-wife.html; Natasha Frost, "Founder of Australia's Hillsong Church Resigns Amid Scandals," *New York Times*, March 23 2022, https://www.nytimes.com/2022/03/23 /world/australia/brian-houston-hillsong-resign.html; Tracy Wright, "Disgraced Celebrity Pastor Carl Lentz Cheated with Family Nanny; Hillsong Church Documentary Details Scandal," Fox News, May 15 2023, https://www.foxnews.com/entertainment /disgraced-celebrity-pastor-carl-lentz-cheated-family-nanny -hillsong-church-documentary-details-scandal; Charity Gibson, "John Gray Addresses Cheating Rumors on 'The Real,' Says He Only Had an 'Emotional Affair,'" *Christian Post*, March 12 2019, https://www.christianpost.com/news/john-gray-addresses -cheating-rumors-on-the-real-says-he-only-had-an-emotional -affair.html; Keydra Manns, "Pastor John Gray 'Publicly Honors' Wife after Cheating Again: 'My Wife Deserves Better,'" The Grio, November 10, 2020, https://thegrio.com/2020/11/10/john- gray-wife-cheating-instagram/; Ruth Graham, "What the Latest Investigations Into Catholic Church Sex Abuse Mean," *New York Times*, June 2, 2023, https://www.nytimes.com/2023/06/02 /us/catholic-church-sex-abuse-investigations.html.

CHAPTER 15: Shhhhh, We're in Church

1   David J. Ayers, "Sex and the Single Evangelical," Institute for Family Studies, August 14, 2019, https://ifstudies.org/blog /sex-and-the-single-evangelical.

2   Adam Gabbatt, "Losing Their Religion: Why US Churches Are
    on the Decline," *The Guardian*, January 22, 2023, https://www
    .theguardian.com/us-news/2023/jan/22/us-churches-closing
    -religion-covid-christianity#:~:text=Some%20of%20the%20
    reasons%20were,or%20hypocritical%2C"%20McConnell%20said.

3   Jason Upton, "Dying Star," 2021, Jason Upton & Key of David
    Ministries, Inc.

4   Joshua Harris, Instagram Post beginning, "My heart is full of
    gratitude," Instagram, July 26 2019, https://www.instagram.com
    /p/B0ZBrNLH2sl/?igsh=YzZhZTZiNWI3Nw==.

5   Ibid.

CHAPTER 18: To Believe or Not to Believe

1   Premier Unbelievable?, "Rod Dreher & Louise Perry •
    Christianity, the Sexual Revolution and the Future of the West,"
    Premier Unbelievable? YouTube channel, April 27, 2023,
    https://www.youtube.com/watch?v=MYf7aHe_GT0.

2   Heather Tomlinson, "Why Feminist Louise Perry Is Arguing for
    the Restoration of Traditional Marriage and Christian Sexual
    Ethics," Premier Unbelievable, May 25, 2023, https://www
    .premierunbelievable.com/articles/why-feminist-louise-perry-is
    -arguing-for-the-restoration-of-traditional-marriage-and-christian
    -sexual-ethics/15602.article.

3   Ibid.

4   Ibid.

CHAPTER 19: Your Purity Song

1 Gary Thomas, "If You Think Purity Culture Was Bad, Just Wait until You Hear about Hook Up Culture," *Simply Sacred with Gary Thomas* (Substack), June 14, 2023, https://garythomasbooks .substack.com/p/if-you-think-purity-culture-was-bad.

2 Ibid.

3 Ibid.

At CGM, we are proud to create media that ministers to the lost while waking up the Church! Shining a light in the darkness for others to find their way home to Jesus is the passion of my life and my work. Like. Subscribe. Share. And when you can—give! Please remember your contributions enable the work of this ministry. www.cynthiagarrett.org